Copyright © 2023 by Sophia M. Johnson (Author)
All rights reserved. No part of this book may be reproduced or utilized in any form or by any means, electronic or mechanical, including photocopying, recording or by any information storage and retrieval system, without permission in writing from the publisher, except for brief quotations in critical articles or reviews.
The content of this book is based on various sources and is intended for educational and entertainment purposes only. While the author has made every effort to ensure the accuracy, completeness, and reliability of the information provided, the information may be subject to errors, omissions, or inaccuracies. Therefore, the author makes no warranties, express or implied, regarding the content of this book.
Readers are advised to seek the guidance of a licensed professional before attempting any techniques or actions outlined in this book. The author is not responsible for any losses, damages, or injuries that may arise from the use of information contained within. The information provided in this book is not intended to be a substitute for professional advice, and readers should not rely solely on the information presented.
By reading this book, readers acknowledge that the author is not providing legal, financial, medical, or professional advice. Any reliance on the information contained in this book is solely at the reader's own risk.

Thank you for selecting this book as a valuable source of knowledge and inspiration. Our aim is to provide you with insights and information that will enrich your understanding and enhance your personal growth. We appreciate your decision to embark on this journey of discovery with us, and we hope that this book will exceed your expectations and leave a lasting impact on your life.

Title: Intentions for Self-Fulfilment: Habits and Practices for Thriving
Subtitle: Movement as Medicine: Yoga and Meditation

Series: Worldwide Wellwishes: Cultural Traditions, Inspirational Journeys and Self-Care Rituals for Fulfillment in the Coming Year
Author: Sophia M. Johnson

Table of Contents

Introduction 5
The Science Behind Transformation 5
Crafting an Envisioned Future Self 9
Sustaining Growth Through Ritual 15

Chapter 1: Writing Down Goals and Affirmations . 22
Enlisting the Brain 22
Being Specific 29
Keeping Accountable 38
Revising When Necessary 48

Chapter 2: Cultivating Gratitude 57
Research on Benefits 57
Morning Reflection Rituals 65
Gratitude Journaling 73
Unexpected Blessings 81

Chapter 3: Practicing Mindfulness 87
Understanding Autopilot Habits 87
Getting Centered Through Meditation 97
Body Scans for Calm Presence 105
Loving-Kindness Toward Self and Others 115

Chapter 4: Fueling Positivity Through Movement 125
Neuroscience of Exercise 125
Yoga Poses for Peace 135
Dance Therapy 144
Laughter as Powerful Medicine 151

Chapter 5: Healthy Eating for Clarity 159
Nutrients for Well-Being 159

Traditional Foods for Grounding *166*
Mindful Cooking and Eating *172*
Nourishing Community *178*
Chapter 6: Creative Expression **184**
Finding Natural Talents *184*
Learning New Skills *190*
Sharing Your Light..*197*
Receiving Others' Gifts *203*
Chapter 7: Touchstones for Reminding Yourself of Purpose **209**
Totems From Nature *209*
Inspirational Quotes *216*
Uplifting Music Playlists *222*
Support Networks *228*
Conclusion **234**
Progress Over Perfection *234*
Flexibility Along the Path..*240*
Transformation as a Continuum *247*
Wordbook **254**
Supplementary Materials **257**

Introduction
The Science Behind Transformation

In the dawn of a new year, as the clock strikes midnight and a fresh calendar page turns, many of us find ourselves standing at the crossroads of reflection and anticipation. It's a moment pregnant with possibilities, a canvas waiting to be painted with the hues of our aspirations and dreams. In this moment of transition, we embark on a journey toward self-fulfillment, armed with the wisdom of the past and the hope of the future.

As we set foot on this path of transformation, it's essential to understand that the pursuit of personal growth is not merely a subjective, whimsical endeavor; there is a profound science behind the process of transformation. In this section, we delve into the neurological, psychological, and physiological aspects that underpin our ability to change, grow, and thrive.

The Science Behind Transformation

Neuroplasticity: The Malleability of the Brain

At the very core of our capacity for transformation lies the marvel of neuroplasticity—the brain's remarkable ability to reorganize itself, both structurally and functionally, in response to experience. This phenomenon challenges the age-old notion that the brain's neural circuits are fixed in adulthood. Instead, research has shown that our brains possess a remarkable degree of plasticity, constantly rewiring and adapting based on our thoughts, behaviors, and experiences.

Understanding neuroplasticity is like discovering the architectural blueprint of personal growth. When we engage in activities such as setting goals, practicing mindfulness, or learning new skills, our brains respond by forging new neural connections. The more we repeat these positive behaviors, the stronger these connections become, ultimately shaping our thoughts, habits, and, consequently, our lives.

The Role of Habits and Routines

As creatures of habit, much of our daily lives is governed by routine. The science of habit formation sheds light on how habits are ingrained in the neural pathways of our brains. Habits, both constructive and destructive, are deeply rooted in the basal ganglia, a region responsible for motor control and procedural learning. Understanding this neural foundation allows us to strategically cultivate habits that align with our aspirations.

In the context of transformational resolutions, breaking down overarching goals into smaller, actionable habits becomes a key strategy. By consistently engaging in these habits, we not only create positive neural pathways but also make the journey of self-improvement more manageable and sustainable.

The Power of Visualization

Visualization serves as a potent tool in the process of transformation, acting as a bridge between thought and action. Neuroscientific research suggests that when we vividly imagine ourselves achieving our goals, the brain interprets this mental imagery as a real experience. This process activates the same neural networks that would be engaged during the actual performance of the task.

By harnessing the power of visualization, we leverage the brain's ability to familiarize itself with success, making the pursuit of our goals feel more attainable. In this way, visualization becomes a catalyst for turning intentions into actions, paving the way for the realization of our envisioned future selves.

The Impact of Positive Psychology

Positive psychology, a field that emerged in the late 20th century, focuses on the study of human flourishing and optimal well-being. Unlike traditional psychology, which often emphasizes pathology and dysfunction, positive psychology explores the factors that contribute to a fulfilling and meaningful life.

One of the cornerstones of positive psychology is the concept of strengths and virtues. By identifying and leveraging our unique strengths, we can cultivate a sense of purpose and fulfillment. Research shows that individuals who utilize their strengths in their daily lives experience higher levels of happiness and life satisfaction.

In the journey of self-fulfillment, positive psychology serves as a guiding light, encouraging us to shift our focus from fixing weaknesses to amplifying strengths. This paradigm shift not only enhances our well-being but also fuels the transformative process by aligning our goals with our innate capacities.

The Physiology of Stress and Resilience

Transformation is not a linear journey; it often involves navigating challenges and setbacks. Understanding the physiology of stress and resilience equips us with tools to navigate these inevitable hurdles.

When faced with stress, our bodies enter a state of physiological arousal known as the "fight or flight" response.

While this response is crucial for survival in acute situations, chronic stress can have detrimental effects on our physical and mental well-being. The release of stress hormones, such as cortisol, can impair cognitive function, weaken the immune system, and contribute to various health issues.

Conversely, cultivating resilience is a key component of successful transformation. Resilience involves adapting to adversity, bouncing back from setbacks, and maintaining psychological well-being in the face of challenges. Research indicates that practices such as mindfulness meditation, social support, and a positive mindset can enhance resilience, fostering a more robust capacity to navigate the ups and downs of the transformational journey.

Navigating the Landscape of Transformation

In weaving the fabric of personal growth, it's essential to recognize that transformation is not a one-size-fits-all endeavor. Each individual's journey is unique, influenced by a myriad of factors including personality, values, and life circumstances. By appreciating the science behind transformation, we gain insights that empower us to tailor our approach, making the journey more personalized, sustainable, and fulfilling.

As we embark on this exploration of intentional living and self-fulfillment, let us carry with us the understanding that our capacity for transformation is rooted in the very fabric of our being—the intricate dance of neurons, the resilience of the mind, and the artistry of positive psychology. In the chapters that follow, we will delve deeper into practical strategies and rituals that harness this science, guiding us toward a more intentional and thriving existence.

Crafting an Envisioned Future Self

In the kaleidoscope of human experience, the concept of a new year serves as a natural demarcation—an opportunity to reflect on the past, embrace the present, and project ourselves into an envisioned future. As we stand at the threshold of change, the canvas of possibility unfurls before us, inviting us to be the architects of our destinies. In this section, we explore the art of crafting an envisioned future self, a process that goes beyond traditional goal-setting and ventures into the realm of intentional living and self-creation.

The Power of Vision

At the heart of crafting an envisioned future self lies the power of vision—a mental image of the person we aspire to become. Unlike mere goals, which can be transactional and short-term, a vision encapsulates the essence of our desired identity and the life we wish to lead. It is a beacon that guides our choices, shapes our priorities, and infuses our daily actions with purpose.

Research in psychology emphasizes the transformative impact of having a clear and compelling vision. When we vividly imagine our future selves, our brains engage in a process akin to mental time travel. This cognitive act not only activates the same neural networks associated with goal pursuit but also aligns our present actions with our future aspirations.

Crafting a vision involves contemplating the various facets of our lives—career, relationships, personal growth, and well-being. It requires us to explore our values, passions, and the impact we wish to have on the world. By creating a detailed and emotionally resonant vision, we set the stage for a holistic and fulfilling transformation.

Values as the North Star

As we embark on the journey of self-crafting, our values serve as the North Star, guiding our decisions and actions. Values are the principles that underpin our sense of meaning and fulfillment. Identifying and aligning with our core values is integral to crafting a future self that is not only successful by external standards but also deeply authentic and satisfying on a personal level.

Consider, for instance, someone who values creativity and autonomy. Their envisioned future self might involve a career that allows for self-expression and the freedom to innovate. By consciously integrating these values into their vision, they create a roadmap that fosters a sense of purpose and joy in their daily endeavors.

Crafting a future self in alignment with our values is akin to constructing a life that resonates with our truest selves. It requires introspection, self-awareness, and the courage to make choices that honor our values, even in the face of external pressures or societal expectations.

Setting Transformational Goals

Goals, when informed by a clear vision, become the stepping stones toward our envisioned future self. However, not all goals are created equal. Transformational goals are those that catalyze significant and positive changes in our lives. They extend beyond the realm of habit or routine and propel us toward the realization of our broader vision.

When setting transformational goals, it's essential to consider the "why" behind each objective. Understanding the deeper purpose and meaning behind our goals enhances motivation and resilience. For example, if the envisioned future self involves a healthier lifestyle, a transformational goal might be to run a marathon. The goal itself becomes a means of embodying the desired identity rather than a mere checklist item.

Moreover, effective transformational goals are often SMART: Specific, Measurable, Achievable, Relevant, and Time-bound. This framework provides a practical structure for translating the abstract vision into actionable steps. By breaking down the journey into smaller, manageable goals, we create a roadmap that is both inspiring and attainable.

The Role of Identity in Transformation

Crafting an envisioned future self goes beyond changing external circumstances; it involves a shift in identity. Our identity—the core sense of who we are—plays a pivotal role in shaping our behaviors and decisions. Transformation becomes more sustainable when it is anchored in a shift in self-perception.

Psychologist Erik Erikson proposed that identity development is a lifelong process, and each stage of life presents an opportunity for refining and redefining our sense of self. When consciously crafting an envisioned future self, we engage in a process of identity construction. We ask ourselves not only what we want to achieve but who we want to become.

This process requires introspection and a willingness to challenge and expand our self-concept. For example, if the envisioned future self involves becoming a more compassionate and empathetic person, the transformation extends beyond behavioral changes—it necessitates a deepening of our sense of empathy and a reframing of how we perceive ourselves in relation to others.

Embracing Growth Mindset

Central to the process of crafting an envisioned future self is the cultivation of a growth mindset—a belief that our abilities and intelligence can be developed through dedication and hard work. A growth mindset fosters resilience in the face of challenges, as setbacks are viewed not as failures but as opportunities for learning and growth.

Psychologist Carol Dweck's research on mindset underscores the impact of our beliefs about learning and intelligence on our behavior. Individuals with a growth mindset are more likely to persevere in the face of difficulties, embrace challenges, and see effort as a path to mastery.

In the context of crafting an envisioned future self, a growth mindset becomes a powerful ally. It encourages us to view the journey of transformation as a dynamic process, where our efforts and dedication contribute to our development. This mindset shift not only enhances our capacity to overcome obstacles but also fosters a sense of agency and control over our own growth.

Visualization Techniques for Self-Crafting

Visualization, a technique often associated with athletes and performers, emerges as a valuable tool in the process of self-crafting. By vividly imagining our envisioned future selves, we activate the brain's neural pathways associated with goal pursuit, creating a mental rehearsal for our desired reality.

Incorporating visualization into our daily routines allows us to reinforce the connection between our present actions and our future aspirations. This practice goes beyond wishful thinking; it involves immersing ourselves in the sensory details of our envisioned success. Whether visualizing a successful presentation at work, a harmonious relationship, or a state of optimal well-being, the act of visualization strengthens the neural blueprint for our desired future.

Accountability and Support Systems

Crafting an envisioned future self is not a solitary endeavor. The journey benefits from accountability and support systems that provide encouragement, guidance, and a sense of shared commitment. Communicating our vision to trusted friends, family, or mentors creates a network of accountability that can help us stay on course, especially when faced with challenges.

Moreover, seeking support from those who have walked a similar path or possess expertise in areas relevant to our vision enhances the likelihood of success. Whether through mentorship, coaching, or community engagement, surrounding ourselves with individuals who champion our growth contributes to the richness and depth of our transformational journey.

Nurturing the Seed of Transformation

As we delve into the intricacies of crafting an envisioned future self, it's crucial to recognize that transformation is not a destination but a continuous process. The seed of change requires nurturing through self-compassion, resilience, and a commitment to lifelong learning. In the chapters that follow, we will explore practical tools, rituals, and habits that align with the principles of intentional living and support the flourishing of our envisioned future selves. Together, let us embark on this transformative journey, weaving the tapestry of our lives with purpose, authenticity, and the unwavering belief in the boundless potential within us.

Sustaining Growth Through Ritual

In the rhythm of our daily lives, the pursuit of personal growth often encounters the ebb and flow of motivation, the challenge of consistency, and the inevitability of obstacles. It is within this dynamic dance that the significance of sustaining growth through ritual becomes apparent. Rituals, infused with intention and mindfulness, serve as the bedrock upon which our transformative journey finds stability and continuity.

The Nature of Rituals

Rituals are more than mere routines; they are symbolic acts that carry personal significance and contribute to a sense of order and meaning in our lives. Rooted in cultural, religious, or personal traditions, rituals have been an integral part of human existence throughout history. In the context of personal growth, rituals take on a purposeful role—they become the threads that weave together our aspirations and daily existence.

Understanding the nature of rituals involves recognizing their power to shape our mindset and behaviors. Unlike spontaneous actions, rituals are deliberate and intentional. They serve as markers in time, signifying the importance of specific moments or activities. Whether it's the act of journaling each morning, practicing gratitude before bedtime, or engaging in a mindful movement routine, rituals create a rhythm that aligns with our values and vision.

The Rituals of Morning: Setting the Tone for the Day

The morning holds a unique space in our daily narrative—a canvas upon which we sketch the initial strokes of our day. Morning rituals, when crafted with intention, have the potential to set a positive tone that ripples through the hours that follow. From the moment we wake, we have the opportunity to shape our mindset, cultivate gratitude, and align ourselves with our goals.

Mindful Awakening: Instead of succumbing to the hurried pace of morning routines, consider cultivating a mindful awakening ritual. This could involve taking a few moments to center yourself before getting out of bed, expressing gratitude for the gift of a new day, and setting positive intentions for the hours ahead. By infusing mindfulness into the first moments of wakefulness, you lay the foundation for a day that unfolds with greater awareness.

Gratitude Practice: Research consistently highlights the transformative effects of gratitude on well-being. Morning rituals that involve expressing gratitude—whether through journaling, reflection, or spoken words—create a lens through which we perceive the world. This intentional focus on the positive aspects of life contributes to a mindset of abundance and appreciation, fostering a more resilient and growth-oriented approach to challenges.

Goal Setting: Mornings provide an opportune time to revisit and refine our goals. By incorporating a brief goal-setting ritual into the early hours, we reaffirm our commitment to personal growth. This could involve reviewing overarching goals, breaking them down into actionable steps, and visualizing the successful achievement of these milestones. Morning goal-setting rituals serve as a compass, directing our actions throughout the day.

The Transformative Power of Daily Reflection

In the tapestry of personal growth, daily reflection emerges as a thread that stitches together our experiences, insights, and aspirations. The act of reflecting on our day, thoughts, and emotions fosters self-awareness, a cornerstone of intentional living. Daily reflection rituals provide a sacred space for introspection, learning, and the refinement of our path toward self-fulfillment.

Journaling as a Reflective Practice: Journaling, a timeless and accessible ritual, offers a canvas for self-expression and exploration. Engaging in reflective journaling at the end of each day allows us to capture the nuances of our experiences, articulate our thoughts and emotions, and identify patterns in our behavior. Through this practice, we gain clarity on our values, progress, and areas for growth.

The Power of Questions: Integrating reflective questions into our daily rituals enhances the depth of our self-inquiry. Questions such as "What brought me joy today?" or "In what ways did I step outside my comfort zone?" prompt a nuanced examination of our experiences. By consistently asking thought-provoking questions, we invite a continuous dialogue with ourselves, unraveling layers of insight and self-discovery.

Evening Rituals for Closure: As the day draws to a close, intentional rituals signal a transition from activity to rest. This could involve a brief meditation, a gratitude practice, or the review of achievements and lessons learned. Evening rituals create a sense of closure, allowing us to release the day's challenges and embrace a mindset of rejuvenation and growth for the days ahead.

Mindful Movement: The Embodiment of Growth

The body, as a vessel of our experiences, plays a profound role in the journey of personal growth. Mindful movement rituals, encompassing practices such as yoga, tai chi, or simply intentional walking, bridge the gap between the physical and the spiritual. These rituals not only contribute to physical well-being but also serve as a medium for self-discovery and embodiment.

Yoga as a Ritual of Connection: Yoga, with its roots in ancient wisdom, has evolved into a modern-day ritual for holistic well-being. The intentional union of breath and movement in yoga fosters a mind-body connection that transcends the confines of the mat. Incorporating a regular yoga practice into our routine becomes a ritual of self-care, promoting flexibility, strength, and a sense of inner calm.

Tai Chi for Flow and Balance: Tai Chi, an ancient Chinese martial art, embodies the principles of balance and flow. This slow and deliberate practice not only enhances physical health but also cultivates a state of mindfulness. As a ritual, Tai Chi becomes a moving meditation, grounding us in the present moment and fostering a harmonious relationship between body and mind.

Walking Meditation: The simple act of walking, when approached with mindfulness, transforms into a ritual of presence and awareness. Walking meditation involves paying attention to each step, the rhythm of breath, and the sensations in the body. Whether practiced in nature or within the urban landscape, walking meditation becomes a ritual that invites us to attune to the present moment, providing a respite from the demands of daily life.

Rituals for Connection and Community

The journey of personal growth is not a solitary expedition; it thrives in the soil of connection and community. Rituals that foster a sense of belonging, empathy, and shared purpose contribute to the richness of our growth-oriented environment.

Group Reflection Circles: Establishing a practice of group reflection circles, whether with friends, family, or like-minded individuals, creates a supportive space for shared insights and collective growth. These circles, guided by reflective prompts, provide an opportunity to learn from one another, celebrate achievements, and offer encouragement during challenges.

Shared Practices: Rituals gain potency when shared with others. Whether it's a weekly book club meeting, a cooking class, or a group meditation session, shared practices create a sense of unity and accountability. Engaging in rituals as a community fosters a collective energy that propels each individual toward their growth aspirations.

Celebratory Rituals: Milestones, both big and small, deserve recognition and celebration. Establishing celebratory rituals—whether it's a monthly reflection on achievements, a gratitude ceremony, or a symbolic gesture of accomplishment—creates a positive feedback loop. These rituals not only acknowledge progress but also infuse joy and motivation into the ongoing journey of personal development.

Culinary Rituals: Nourishing the Body and Soul

The act of nourishing ourselves goes beyond the functional aspect of sustenance; it is a ritual that carries the potential for mindfulness, gratitude, and connection.

Culinary rituals, involving the preparation and consumption of food, become a sensorial experience that nurtures both the body and the soul.

Mindful Eating Practices: In a fast-paced world, meals are often consumed hurriedly, without attention to the sensory experience of eating. Mindful eating rituals invite us to savor each bite, appreciate the flavors and textures, and cultivate gratitude for the nourishment provided by the food. By transforming mealtime into a mindful ritual, we deepen our connection to the act of nourishment.

Cooking as a Creative Ritual: The process of preparing meals can be a creative and meditative ritual. Whether it's experimenting with new recipes, sourcing fresh ingredients, or infusing love into the cooking process, culinary rituals become an opportunity to express creativity and engage in a form of self-care.

Shared Meals as Bonding Rituals: The act of sharing a meal transcends the physical act of eating; it is a ritual of communion and connection. Establishing shared meal rituals with friends, family, or colleagues fosters a sense of belonging and strengthens social bonds. The conversations and shared experiences during these meals contribute to the tapestry of our growth journey.

Embracing Rituals as Guardians of Growth

In the symphony of personal growth, rituals emerge as guardians that stand sentinel, protecting the flame of intention and purpose. They infuse our lives with a sense of order, rhythm, and sacredness. Whether morning rituals that set the tone for the day, reflective practices that deepen self-awareness, mindful movements that connect us to our bodies, or communal rituals that foster connection, each ritual contributes to the sustainability and depth of our growth journey.

As we delve into the exploration of sustaining growth through ritual, let us remember that rituals are not rigid prescriptions but adaptable expressions of our evolving selves. They are the compass and the anchor, guiding us through the currents of change and offering solace in moments of uncertainty. In the chapters that follow, we will continue to unravel the rich tapestry of intentional living, exploring practical tools and wisdom that align with the principles of sustained growth and fulfillment. Together, let us embrace rituals as companions on the journey to becoming our best selves.

Chapter 1: Writing Down Goals and Affirmations Enlisting the Brain

In the symphony of self-transformation, the act of setting goals and affirmations serves as the overture—a deliberate and powerful commencement that echoes the aspirations of our envisioned future selves. As we embark on this chapter dedicated to the art of writing down goals and affirmations, it's essential to explore the intricate dance between our intentions and the orchestrator of our actions—the brain.

The Cognitive Blueprint: How Writing Shapes Thought

The act of writing is not a mere transcription of thoughts onto paper; it is an act of cognitive creation, a process that engages various regions of the brain to sculpt and solidify our aspirations. Understanding the cognitive blueprint of writing allows us to appreciate its transformative impact on our mindset and behavior.

The Power of Externalization: When we commit our goals and affirmations to paper, we externalize the abstract realm of thought into a tangible form. This externalization is not a passive act; it is an engagement with the motor and visual cortex of the brain. The physical act of forming letters, words, and sentences signals to the brain that our intentions are concrete and worthy of attention.

Research in psychology, including studies conducted by Dr. Gail Matthews at Dominican University of California, has consistently demonstrated the efficacy of writing down goals. The act of externalizing goals enhances clarity, commitment, and the likelihood of goal attainment. It transforms nebulous aspirations into concrete plans, providing a roadmap for our journey of growth.

The Reticular Activating System (RAS): A Goal-Seeking Mechanism: Deep within the brain lies the Reticular Activating System, a network of neurons responsible for filtering and prioritizing sensory information. When we commit our goals to writing, we activate the RAS, signaling to the brain that these goals are of particular importance.

Consider the RAS as a selective focus lens. When you decide on a specific goal and write it down, the RAS heightens your awareness of relevant opportunities and resources in your environment. It's the reason why, after deciding to buy a particular car, you suddenly start noticing that car everywhere—it's not that there are more of them; your RAS is now attuned to that specific information.

By enlisting the RAS through the act of writing down goals, we create a mental filter that sifts through the vast sea of stimuli, amplifying our awareness of opportunities aligned with our aspirations. This cognitive mechanism becomes an ally in the pursuit of our envisioned future self.

The Psychology of Commitment: Inked Intentions

Writing down goals transcends the realm of a mere to-do list; it is a commitment ceremony, an affirmation to ourselves and the universe that these aspirations hold significance in our journey. The psychology of commitment plays a pivotal role in transforming goals from fleeting thoughts to enduring pursuits.

Public Commitment vs. Private Commitment: The act of writing down goals is a private commitment to oneself, a personal covenant that echoes within the corridors of the mind. However, the power of public commitment should not be underestimated. Sharing our goals with trusted friends, family, or mentors adds an extra layer of accountability.

Studies on goal-setting and commitment, such as the work of Dr. Peter Gollwitzer, highlight the impact of sharing goals with others. Publicly stating our intentions creates a social contract, elevating the stakes of our commitment. The fear of falling short in the eyes of others becomes a motivational force, propelling us to align our actions with our declared aspirations.

The Zeigarnik Effect: Unfinished Business in the Mind: The Zeigarnik Effect, named after psychologist Bluma Zeigarnik, underscores the psychological phenomenon where uncompleted or interrupted tasks occupy a special place in our cognitive landscape. When we write down goals, we initiate a mental loop—a persistent reminder in the background of our consciousness that these objectives remain unfinished.

This phenomenon becomes a catalyst for action. The brain, wired to seek closure, compels us to take steps toward completing the tasks we've set for ourselves. The act of writing down goals, therefore, initiates a dynamic interplay between intention and action, creating a psychological tension that propels us forward.

Specificity and Clarity: The Language of the Brain

The brain thrives on clarity and specificity. Vague, ambiguous goals are akin to navigating a foggy terrain, while clear, specific goals act as guiding stars illuminating our path. When we write down goals with precision, we speak the language of the brain, enhancing the likelihood of successful translation from intention to action.

SMART Goals: A Blueprint for Clarity: The SMART criteria—Specific, Measurable, Achievable, Relevant, and Time-bound—provide a framework for crafting goals that resonate with the brain's preference for specificity. Specific goals define the who, what, where, when, and why of our aspirations, offering a clear roadmap for execution.

For example, a vague goal like "lose weight" becomes more actionable when transformed into a SMART goal: "Lose 10 pounds in the next eight weeks by exercising for 30 minutes five times a week and adopting a balanced, plant-based diet." The brain interprets the specificity of this goal as a set of instructions, making it more likely to engage in the necessary behaviors.

Imagery and Visualization: The brain processes visual information with remarkable efficiency. When we write down goals, incorporating vivid imagery and visualization amplifies the impact on the brain's neural circuits. Visualizing the successful attainment of our goals activates the same brain regions that would be engaged during the actual performance of the tasks.

Consider creating a visual representation of your goals—whether through vision boards, mind maps, or drawings. The brain interprets these visual cues as directives, enhancing motivation and creating a mental image of the desired outcome. Visualization, when combined with the act of writing, becomes a potent tool for embedding our goals in the neural architecture of the brain.

Affirmations: Rewiring Neural Pathways

Affirmations, akin to the verses of a personal anthem, are positive statements that articulate our desired beliefs or outcomes. When we write down affirmations, we engage in a process of cognitive rewiring, sculpting neural pathways that shape our self-perception and influence our actions.

Positive Self-Talk and Self-Efficacy: Affirmations serve as a vehicle for positive self-talk, a dialogue with ourselves that fosters self-efficacy and resilience. When we repeatedly write down and affirm positive statements about our abilities and potential, we stimulate the brain's reward centers.

Research in neuroscience, including studies conducted by Dr. Tali Sharot at University College London, suggests that positive affirmations can influence the brain's reward system, reinforcing a positive self-image. This neurological response contributes to an enhanced sense of self-efficacy—the belief in our ability to achieve our goals.

Neuroplasticity and Affirmative Rewiring: The brain's capacity for neuroplasticity—the ability to reorganize and adapt by forming new neural connections—provides a scientific foundation for the efficacy of affirmations. When we consistently write down and repeat positive affirmations, we initiate a process of rewiring neural pathways associated with self-beliefs.

For example, if the affirmation is "I am confident and capable in challenging situations," the repetition of this statement strengthens the neural connections related to confidence. Over time, the brain prioritizes these pathways, influencing our thoughts, emotions, and behaviors.

Affirmations, therefore, become a deliberate act of shaping the neural landscape of our mindset.

The Ritual of Regular Review: Reinforcement and Adjustment

The act of writing down goals and affirmations is not a one-time event; it is a dynamic process that benefits from regular review and refinement. The brain, with its capacity for adaptation, responds to ongoing reinforcement and allows us to make informed adjustments to our aspirations.

Reflection and Adjustment: Regularly reviewing written goals provides an opportunity for reflection. What progress have we made? What challenges have we encountered? This reflective process allows us to celebrate achievements, learn from setbacks, and make informed adjustments to our goals.

When we acknowledge and celebrate progress, the brain experiences a release of dopamine, a neurotransmitter associated with pleasure and reward. This neurochemical response strengthens the neural pathways associated with goal pursuit, creating a positive feedback loop that enhances motivation.

Adapting to Changing Priorities: Life is dynamic, and priorities may shift over time. The ritual of regular goal review allows us to align our aspirations with evolving circumstances and values. It provides the flexibility to discard goals that no longer resonate and embrace new objectives that align with our current vision.

The brain's ability to adapt to changing circumstances, known as cognitive flexibility, is crucial for sustained growth. By regularly reassessing and adjusting our written goals, we tap into the brain's inherent capacity for adaptation, ensuring that our aspirations remain relevant and inspiring.

Writing Down Goals and Affirmations: A Symphony of Intention

In the orchestration of personal growth, the act of writing down goals and affirmations emerges as a symphony of intention—a harmonious blend of cognitive engagement, commitment, specificity, and ongoing refinement. By enlisting the brain in this creative process, we harness the neurobiological mechanisms that shape our thoughts, beliefs, and actions.

As we delve deeper into the subsequent chapters, each note in the symphony resonates with intention, contributing to the richness and depth of our transformative journey. Writing down goals and affirmations becomes not only a ritual of personal commitment but also a partnership with the brain—a collaborative endeavor that aligns our inner orchestra with the external melodies of our envisioned future self. Together, let us continue to explore the intricacies of intentional living, each written goal and affirmation serving as a musical note in the grand composition of our growth.

Being Specific

In the realm of personal growth, the difference between a vague aspiration and a concrete, achievable goal lies in the art of specificity. Being specific is akin to charting a clear course on the map of our intentions, providing the guidance necessary to navigate the terrain of transformation. In this exploration of specificity within the context of writing down goals and affirmations, we uncover the nuanced layers that transform mere aspirations into actionable blueprints for success.

The Power of Precision

At the heart of being specific is the power of precision—the art of articulating our aspirations with clarity, detail, and unambiguous language. Specificity serves as the compass that directs our efforts, allowing us to navigate the vast landscape of personal growth with purpose and determination.

Clarity in Purpose: When we set specific goals, we provide our minds with a crystal-clear target. Imagine an archer aiming at a vague outline versus a distinct bullseye. The specificity of the target enhances the precision of the shot. Similarly, when our goals are clear and specific, our efforts become more targeted, increasing the likelihood of hitting the mark.

Psychologically, clarity in purpose activates the brain's prefrontal cortex, the region responsible for decision-making, goal-setting, and strategic planning. Specific goals engage the brain in a cognitive process akin to problem-solving, creating a roadmap for action.

Transforming Ambiguity into Action: Ambiguity in goal-setting often leads to procrastination and indecision. Vague goals, such as "get fit" or "save money," lack the specificity necessary for actionable steps. The brain, when faced with ambiguous directives, may default to the familiar and routine, impeding progress.

Being specific transforms ambiguity into action. Consider the difference between the vague goal "exercise more" and its specific counterpart "run three times a week for 30 minutes." The latter provides a clear framework, eliminating ambiguity and offering a tangible plan of action. This specificity propels the brain into a mode of task initiation, initiating the cascade of behaviors required for goal attainment.

The SMART Framework: Blueprint for Specificity

In the realm of goal-setting, the SMART framework stands as a guiding beacon for specificity. SMART, an acronym for Specific, Measurable, Achievable, Relevant, and Time-bound, encapsulates the essential elements that transform goals from abstract aspirations into concrete and actionable plans.

Specificity in the "S" of SMART: The first element of the SMART framework, specificity, sets the foundation for the entire goal-setting process. Specific goals answer the fundamental questions of what, why, and how. What exactly do I want to achieve? Why is this goal important to me? How will I accomplish it?

For example, consider the goal "Improve my financial situation." While the intention is positive, it lacks specificity. Applying the "S" of SMART transforms it into "Save $5,000 in the next six months by creating a monthly budget and reducing non-essential expenses." The specificity in this refined goal provides a clear roadmap, outlining the specific amount, timeframe, and actionable steps.

Measurable Progress: Specific goals naturally lend themselves to measurement. The "M" in SMART ensures that our goals are quantifiable, allowing us to track progress and celebrate achievements. Measuring progress provides feedback to the brain, reinforcing the sense of accomplishment and motivating continued effort.

Returning to the financial goal example, the measurable aspect could involve tracking monthly savings, creating a visual chart, or using budgeting tools to monitor expenditures. Measurable progress not only enhances motivation but also enables us to make informed adjustments to our strategies.

Specificity in Goal Language

Beyond the SMART framework, the language we use to articulate our goals plays a crucial role in achieving specificity. Specific goals are characterized by precision, clarity, and an absence of ambiguity. Here are key elements to consider when crafting specific goals:

Define the What: Clearly articulate what you want to achieve. Instead of a broad statement like "improve health," specify the aspect you aim to address, such as "lose 10 pounds," "lower cholesterol by 20 points," or "increase flexibility."

Identify the Why: Attach a meaningful purpose or rationale to your goal. Understanding the significance of a goal enhances motivation. For instance, instead of a generic fitness goal, you might specify, "Lose 10 pounds to improve overall well-being and energy levels, reducing the risk of lifestyle-related health issues."

Break Down Complex Goals: If your overarching goal is complex, break it down into smaller, more manageable components. This not only enhances clarity but also facilitates a step-by-step approach to achievement. For example, if your goal is to "start a business," break it down into specific steps like "research business ideas," "create a business plan," and "register the business."

Quantify When Possible: Where applicable, use quantifiable metrics to define your goals. This adds a layer of precision and facilitates measurement. For instance, instead of a generic goal like "save money," specify an amount, such as "save $1,000 by the end of the quarter."

Include Action Steps: Outline specific actions you will take to achieve your goals. This transforms abstract intentions into actionable plans. For a goal like "improve time management," specify actions such as "create a daily schedule," "prioritize tasks," and "minimize multitasking."

Consider Potential Obstacles: Anticipate potential obstacles and challenges. While not directly related to specificity, addressing potential barriers in your goal language demonstrates a thoughtful and realistic approach. For instance, if your goal is to "exercise five times a week," consider adding, "overcoming scheduling conflicts by planning workouts in advance."

Case Studies in Specificity

To illustrate the transformative power of specificity, let's delve into a couple of case studies, examining how the refinement of vague goals into specific, actionable plans can significantly impact the trajectory of personal growth.

Case Study 1: Career Advancement

Vague Goal: "Advance in my career."

Specific Goal: "Attain a promotion to the position of Senior Project Manager within the next 12 months by completing an advanced project management certification, leading two successful cross-functional projects, and consistently exceeding performance targets."

In this case, the specificity of the goal shifts the focus from a broad desire for career advancement to a targeted plan of action. The inclusion of specific actions—earning a certification, leading projects, and exceeding performance targets—provides a clear roadmap for advancement.

Case Study 2: Health and Fitness

Vague Goal: "Get in shape."

Specific Goal: "Achieve a body fat percentage of 18% within six months by following a structured workout routine (weightlifting three times a week and cardio twice a week), adopting a nutrition plan focused on lean proteins and vegetables, and tracking progress bi-weekly."

The specificity in this health and fitness goal transforms a generic aspiration into a concrete plan. By defining the desired body fat percentage, outlining a specific workout routine and nutrition plan, and incorporating a measurable tracking mechanism, the goal becomes actionable and achievable.

Case Study 3: Financial Management

Vague Goal: "Save money."

Specific Goal: "Build an emergency fund of $3,000 within the next nine months by setting aside $300 from each paycheck, eliminating non-essential monthly subscriptions, and creating a budget to track and minimize discretionary spending."

This financial goal exemplifies specificity by quantifying the savings target, outlining specific actions (allocating a specific amount from each paycheck, cutting non-essential expenses), and incorporating a measurable element through budget tracking.

Overcoming Challenges in Specificity

While specificity is a powerful tool in goal-setting, challenges may arise in its application. Here are common challenges and strategies to overcome them:

Fear of Commitment: Some individuals may hesitate to be specific due to a fear of commitment. The idea of setting specific goals with clear parameters can be intimidating. To overcome this, recognize that specificity enhances clarity and commitment, providing a roadmap without stifling adaptability.

Uncertainty About the Future: Future uncertainties can make it challenging to set specific goals. In such cases, focus on what you can control in the present. Set short-term, specific goals that align with your current understanding and adjust as circumstances evolve.

Perfectionism: The desire for perfection can hinder specificity, as individuals may fear setting goals that they may not achieve flawlessly. Embrace the concept of progress over perfection. Specific goals are not about achieving perfection but about making tangible progress toward a desired outcome.

Overwhelm: The complexity of a goal may lead to overwhelm, causing individuals to shy away from specificity. Break down complex goals into smaller, manageable steps. Each specific step contributes to the overall achievement of the larger goal.

The Neurological Impact of Specificity

The neurological impact of setting specific goals is profound, influencing cognitive processes, motivation, and decision-making. Here's a closer look at how specificity engages the brain:

Activation of Goal-Oriented Networks: Specific goals activate goal-oriented networks in the brain, including the prefrontal cortex. This engagement enhances cognitive functions related to planning, decision-making, and task initiation.

Dopaminergic Reward System: The brain's reward system, primarily regulated by the neurotransmitter dopamine, responds to the achievement of goals. Specific goals with measurable outcomes trigger dopamine release, reinforcing positive behaviors and motivating continued effort.

Reduction of Decision Fatigue: Specific goals reduce decision fatigue by providing a clear framework for action. Instead of facing numerous choices, individuals can focus on executing the specific steps outlined in their goal plans.

Enhanced Motivation and Commitment: Clarity in purpose, a hallmark of specific goals, enhances motivation and commitment. The brain interprets specific goals as meaningful and achievable, contributing to sustained effort over time.

Crafting Affirmations with Specificity

The principles of specificity extend beyond goal-setting to the realm of affirmations. When crafting affirmations, specificity amplifies their impact, influencing thought patterns and beliefs with greater precision.

Vague Affirmation: "I am successful."

Specific Affirmation: "I am consistently exceeding sales targets at my job, receiving positive feedback from clients, and steadily advancing in my career."

In the specific affirmation, success is defined with clarity, incorporating measurable outcomes and specific actions. This level of detail enhances the affirmation's efficacy in shaping beliefs and attitudes.

Vague Affirmation: "I am healthy."

Specific Affirmation: "I am prioritizing my health by engaging in regular physical activity, nourishing my body with whole foods, and cultivating habits that contribute to my overall well-being."

The specific affirmation provides a clear picture of health-related actions, making it more impactful in reinforcing positive behaviors and beliefs about well-being.

Integrating Specificity into Daily Practices

To harness the power of specificity, integrate the following practices into your daily routine:

Morning Visualization: Begin your day by visualizing the specific actions you will take to move closer to your goals. Envision the steps, the challenges you may encounter, and your successful navigation through them.

Daily Goal Review: Set aside time each day to review your specific goals. Reflect on the progress made, identify any adjustments needed, and reaffirm your commitment to the specific actions outlined in your plan.

Visual Reminders: Create visual reminders of your specific goals and place them in prominent locations. Whether it's a vision board, a written list, or digital reminders, visual cues reinforce the specificity of your intentions.

Check-In Rituals: Establish regular check-in rituals to assess your progress. These rituals may involve journaling, self-reflection, or discussions with accountability partners. The specificity of these check-ins adds a layer of accountability and self-awareness.

Conclusion: The Precision of Progress

In the tapestry of personal growth, specificity emerges as the brushstroke that defines the contours of our aspirations. Being specific is not a constraint but a liberation—a deliberate choice to articulate our goals with clarity, precision, and purpose. As we navigate the landscape of transformation, let us embrace the power of specificity as a compass that guides our actions, a beacon that illuminates the path of progress, and a catalyst that transforms intentions into tangible achievements.

In the chapters to come, each specific goal becomes a catalyst for progress, each articulated affirmation a beacon of empowerment. Together, let us continue to explore the facets of intentional living, with specificity as our ally in the dynamic journey of becoming our best selves.

Keeping Accountable

In the symphony of personal growth, the resonance of accountability forms a vital chord, echoing through the corridors of commitment and echoing the melody of progress. As we delve into the intricacies of writing down goals and affirmations, the concept of keeping accountable emerges as a linchpin—an essential element that transforms intentions into tangible outcomes. In this exploration, we unravel the layers of accountability, understanding its significance, unraveling the science behind its effectiveness, and discovering practical strategies to weave it into the fabric of our transformative journey.

The Essence of Accountability

At its core, accountability is the state of being answerable for one's actions, decisions, and commitments. It is the bridge between intention and realization, the force that propels us from the realm of aspirations to the terrain of achievement. Understanding the essence of accountability involves recognizing its multifaceted nature and appreciating its role as a catalyst for personal growth.

Internal and External Accountability: Accountability takes dual forms—internal and external. Internal accountability is the commitment we make to ourselves, the intrinsic drive to honor our promises and pursue our goals. External accountability, on the other hand, involves the involvement of external factors or individuals that hold us answerable—whether it's a mentor, a friend, a coach, or a community.

Intrinsic Motivation: At its essence, accountability is intertwined with motivation. The intrinsic motivation that stems from personal values, desires, and aspirations is the driving force behind internal accountability. It is the self-generated impetus that fuels our commitment to the goals we set.

The Power of Commitment Devices: In behavioral economics, commitment devices are mechanisms or strategies individuals use to lock in their intentions and overcome self-control problems. Examples include public declarations of goals, financial incentives tied to achievements, or tools that restrict certain behaviors. These devices serve as external sources of accountability, creating structures that support our internal commitment.

The Science Behind Accountability

To appreciate the effectiveness of accountability, it's insightful to delve into the scientific underpinnings that validate its impact on behavior and goal attainment. The interplay of psychological, neurological, and social factors contributes to the efficacy of accountability mechanisms.

Cognitive Dissonance: Psychologically, the concept of cognitive dissonance plays a pivotal role in accountability. Cognitive dissonance is the discomfort that arises when individuals hold conflicting beliefs or attitudes. When we commit to a goal but fail to take aligned actions, cognitive dissonance emerges, creating internal tension.

Accountability acts as a mechanism to resolve cognitive dissonance. By involving external factors or individuals, we introduce a form of external pressure that aligns with our internal commitment. The discomfort of dissonance motivates us to harmonize our actions with our intentions, reducing the incongruence between what we aim to achieve and our actual behaviors.

Social Influence and Norms: Human behavior is profoundly influenced by social factors. The desire for social approval and conformity to social norms are powerful motivators. Accountability mechanisms that involve sharing goals with others or participating in communities where goals are discussed leverage the social influence aspect.

When we commit to our goals publicly or within a supportive community, the fear of social judgment or the desire for positive recognition becomes a compelling force. The alignment with social norms—whether it's a fitness challenge, a book club, or a professional development group—creates a shared context that reinforces commitment and accountability.

Neurological Reward System: The brain's reward system, particularly the release of neurotransmitters like dopamine, plays a crucial role in accountability. When we receive positive feedback, recognition, or a sense of accomplishment related to our goals, the brain experiences a surge in dopamine. This neurochemical response strengthens the neural pathways associated with goal pursuit, creating a positive feedback loop.

Accountability mechanisms that provide regular feedback, celebrate milestones, or offer tangible rewards tap into the brain's reward system. By linking the achievement of goals with positive reinforcement, accountability becomes a neurologically rewarding experience that enhances motivation and perseverance.

Temporal Discounting and Immediate Consequences: Temporal discounting refers to the tendency of individuals to undervalue future rewards in favor of immediate gratification. Accountability mechanisms introduce immediate consequences or rewards tied to our actions, mitigating the impact of temporal discounting.

For example, financial incentives, such as depositing money into a savings account for each completed goal, create immediate consequences that align with long-term objectives. The introduction of immediate accountability bridges the gap between future aspirations and present actions, making the pursuit of goals more tangible and immediate.

Internal Accountability: Cultivating Intrinsic Motivation

While external accountability mechanisms are valuable, the foundation of sustained commitment lies in cultivating internal accountability—nurturing the intrinsic motivation that fuels our pursuit of goals. Here are key strategies to enhance internal accountability:

Clarify Values and Purpose: Connect your goals to your core values and overarching life purpose. When goals align with what truly matters to you, they become more meaningful and intrinsically motivating.

Visualize Success: Regularly engage in visualization exercises where you vividly imagine the successful attainment of your goals. Visualization activates the brain's neural circuits associated with goal achievement, reinforcing your internal commitment.

Set Intrinsic Rewards: Identify intrinsic rewards tied to the accomplishment of your goals. These rewards may include a sense of accomplishment, increased self-esteem, or the fulfillment of personal values. Recognize and celebrate these intrinsic rewards as integral aspects of goal attainment.

Develop Self-Compassion: Internal accountability thrives in an environment of self-compassion. Acknowledge that setbacks are a natural part of the growth journey and treat yourself with kindness and understanding. Self-compassion enhances resilience and sustains internal motivation.

Practice Mindfulness: Cultivate mindfulness to stay attuned to your thoughts, emotions, and actions. Mindfulness fosters self-awareness, helping you recognize when your behaviors align with your intentions and when adjustments are needed.

External Accountability: Leveraging Social Dynamics

External accountability mechanisms leverage social dynamics to reinforce commitment and progress. Whether through partnerships, communities, or mentors, external accountability provides a supportive framework for goal pursuit. Here are effective strategies to harness external accountability:

Accountability Partnerships: Forming partnerships with individuals who share similar goals creates a mutual accountability system. Regular check-ins, goal-sharing sessions, and collaborative problem-solving enhance the sense of shared commitment.

Public Commitment: Publicly declaring your goals, whether through social media, blogs, or community forums, introduces a layer of external accountability. The awareness that others are aware of your intentions creates a sense of responsibility.

Community Engagement: Joining goal-oriented communities or groups provides a supportive environment. The shared experiences, encouragement, and feedback within a community contribute to a sense of accountability. Whether it's a fitness class, a writing group, or an online community, the collective pursuit of goals enhances motivation.

Coaching and Mentorship: Engaging with a coach or mentor introduces structured accountability. The guidance, feedback, and encouragement provided by a coach contribute to a sense of external accountability. Regular sessions create a rhythm of accountability that sustains momentum.

Regular Progress Updates: Establishing a routine of regular progress updates, whether through written reflections, verbal discussions, or visual representations, adds a layer of external accountability. The act of reporting progress fosters a sense of responsibility to stay on track.

Tools and Techniques for Accountability

In addition to understanding the psychological and social dynamics of accountability, practical tools and techniques enhance its implementation in daily life. These tools serve as enablers, providing structure and support for sustained commitment.

Goal Tracking Systems: Utilize goal tracking systems, whether digital apps, journals, or visual charts, to monitor progress. Tracking systems provide a visual representation of your journey, making it easier to identify trends, celebrate achievements, and course-correct as needed.

Daily or Weekly Check-Ins: Establish a routine of daily or weekly check-ins to review your goals. Use this time for self-reflection, assessing your actions, identifying challenges, and strategizing for the upcoming days or weeks.

SMART Goals: Ensure that your goals adhere to the SMART criteria—Specific, Measurable, Achievable, Relevant, and Time-bound. The SMART framework provides a clear structure that facilitates accountability, as each element contributes to a comprehensive plan of action.

Accountability Contracts: Create written or verbal contracts outlining your commitments, consequences for non-compliance, and rewards for achievement. Accountability contracts serve as personal agreements that enhance commitment and clarity.

Incentive Systems: Introduce incentive systems tied to your goals. Whether it's a reward for completing a milestone, a consequence for falling behind, or a system of earned privileges, incentives add a layer of immediate consequences to your actions.

Feedback Loops: Establish feedback loops that provide regular input on your progress. This could involve seeking feedback from accountability partners, mentors, or using self-assessment tools. Feedback loops contribute to continuous improvement and refinement of your goals.

Visual Reminders: Place visual reminders of your goals in prominent locations. Whether it's a vision board, a written list, or digital reminders, visual cues reinforce the accountability tied to your aspirations.

Case Studies in Accountability

To illustrate the diverse ways accountability can be implemented, let's explore case studies showcasing individuals who successfully integrated accountability into their personal growth journeys.

Case Study 1: Fitness Accountability

Vague Goal: "Exercise regularly."

Specific Goal: "Complete a 12-week fitness program that includes strength training three times a week, cardio twice a week, and yoga once a week."

Accountability Mechanisms:

1. Accountability Partner: Partnered with a friend who shared similar fitness goals. They committed to regular check-ins, joint workouts, and shared progress updates.

2. Public Commitment: Posted weekly updates on social media, sharing both successes and challenges. The public commitment created a sense of external accountability.

3. Goal Tracking App: Used a fitness app to track workouts, set reminders, and visualize progress. The app served as a digital accountability tool.

Outcome: By leveraging both internal motivation (intrinsic desire for improved fitness) and external accountability (partnership, public commitment, technology), the individual successfully completed the 12-week program. The combination of social support, regular tracking, and public commitment contributed to sustained motivation and goal attainment.

Case Study 2: Career Advancement

Vague Goal: "Advance in my career."

Specific Goal: "Attain a leadership position within my organization by completing a leadership development program, leading a high-impact project, and networking with senior leaders."

Accountability Mechanisms:

1. Mentorship: Engaged with a mentor who provided guidance on the leadership development program, offered insights on project leadership, and facilitated introductions to senior leaders.

2. Regular Check-Ins: Scheduled monthly check-ins with the mentor to discuss progress, challenges, and adjustments to the career advancement plan.

3. Networking Events: Committed to attending at least one networking event per month to expand professional connections and gain exposure to senior leaders.

Outcome: The integration of mentorship, regular check-ins, and external networking contributed to the individual's successful career advancement. The combination of internal commitment (intrinsic motivation for career growth) and external accountability mechanisms created a synergistic approach to goal attainment.

Overcoming Accountability Challenges

While accountability is a powerful catalyst for goal achievement, challenges may arise in its implementation. Recognizing and addressing these challenges is essential for creating sustainable accountability structures:

Challenge: Procrastination and Resistance Strategy: Break goals into smaller tasks and set specific deadlines for each. Utilize the Pomodoro Technique or time-blocking to create focused work intervals.

Challenge: Lack of Motivation Strategy: Reconnect with the intrinsic motivation behind your goals. Clarify the values and purpose driving your aspirations. Engage in activities that reignite passion and enthusiasm.

Challenge: Overcoming Setbacks Strategy: Embrace setbacks as opportunities for learning and growth. Adjust your approach, seek support from accountability partners, and celebrate the progress made, no matter how small.

Challenge: Accountability Fatigue Strategy: Diversify your accountability mechanisms to avoid monotony. Rotate accountability partners, vary check-in formats, and explore new tools or techniques to keep the process engaging.

Conclusion: The Dance of Commitment

In the grand dance of personal growth, accountability is the partner that gracefully guides us through the steps of commitment, progress, and achievement. Whether through internal motivation or external support, the dance of accountability transforms goals from fleeting intentions into enduring realities.

As we continue our journey through the subsequent chapters, let accountability be the rhythm that propels us forward—a rhythm that harmonizes the beats of intention, action, and fulfillment. Each check-in, each shared goal, and each moment of reflection becomes a step in this intricate dance, a testament to the power of accountability in the symphony of self-transformation. Together, let us waltz through the chapters to come, each one an exploration of the intricate steps that lead us toward our envisioned future selves.

Revising When Necessary

In the dynamic landscape of personal growth, the journey of writing down goals and affirmations is not a rigid, unyielding path but rather a fluid, adaptable exploration. The ability to revise when necessary is a cornerstone of effective goal-setting, allowing us to navigate changing circumstances, evolving priorities, and the inherent twists and turns of life. In this chapter, we delve into the art and science of revising goals and affirmations—understanding when adjustments are needed, embracing the process of refinement, and harnessing the power of flexibility on the transformative journey.

The Evolution of Aspirations

As we embark on the journey of setting goals and affirmations, it's crucial to acknowledge that aspirations are not static entities. They are living, breathing expressions of our desires, subject to the ebb and flow of life's complexities. The evolution of aspirations is influenced by various factors, including personal growth, external circumstances, changing priorities, and newfound insights.

Personal Growth: As we evolve personally, our aspirations naturally transform. What may have been a compelling goal at one stage of life might no longer resonate as we gain new experiences, insights, and understanding. Revising goals allows us to align our aspirations with our evolving sense of self.

External Circumstances: The external landscape, including economic conditions, societal changes, or unforeseen events, can impact the feasibility or relevance of certain goals. The ability to adapt our aspirations in response to external circumstances is a skill that enhances resilience and agility.

Changing Priorities: Life is a mosaic of shifting priorities—career, relationships, health, and personal development. Revising goals enables us to recalibrate our focus based on current priorities, ensuring that our efforts are directed toward what matters most in the present moment.

Newfound Insights: The journey of self-discovery often brings forth new insights and perspectives. These revelations may prompt a reevaluation of our goals and affirmations, inviting us to refine our aspirations in light of deeper self-awareness and understanding.

Recognizing the Need for Revision

While the commitment to our goals is commendable, it's equally important to cultivate the discernment to recognize when revision is necessary. Certain indicators and reflections can serve as guideposts, signaling the opportune moments to reassess and refine our aspirations.

Stagnation or Frustration: If progress toward a particular goal feels stagnant or consistently leads to frustration, it may be a sign that the goal needs revisiting. Stagnation can stem from various factors, such as unrealistic expectations, changing circumstances, or a misalignment between the goal and personal values.

Alignment with Values: Our values serve as the compass guiding our aspirations. If a goal begins to feel incongruent with our core values or if a shift in values occurs, revising the goal becomes a means of realigning our aspirations with our authentic self.

Changed Circumstances: Life is inherently unpredictable, and circumstances can change unexpectedly. Whether it's a career shift, a relocation, or a significant life event, adapting our goals to accommodate changed circumstances is an exercise in practicality and resilience.

Emotional Disconnect: Goals that once sparked enthusiasm may lose their emotional resonance over time. If a goal no longer elicits passion, joy, or a sense of purpose, revising it allows us to reconnect with aspirations that genuinely inspire and motivate us.

Embracing the Process of Refinement

The process of revising goals and affirmations is not an admission of failure but a demonstration of adaptability, self-awareness, and a commitment to authentic growth. Embracing the art of refinement involves a mindset that values progress over perfection, acknowledges the fluid nature of aspirations, and recognizes that the journey is as significant as the destination.

Cultivating a Growth Mindset: A growth mindset perceives challenges and setbacks as opportunities for learning and improvement. Viewing the revision of goals through the lens of a growth mindset allows us to appreciate the insights gained, the lessons learned, and the adaptive nature of personal development.

Learning from Setbacks: Setbacks are an inherent part of any transformative journey. When a goal encounters obstacles or proves challenging to attain, rather than perceiving it as a roadblock, consider it a valuable source of information. What can be learned from the experience, and how can that knowledge inform the revision of goals?

Celebrating Progress: The revision of goals provides an opportunity to celebrate progress made along the journey. Each step forward, regardless of the ultimate destination, is a testament to resilience, determination, and the commitment to personal growth.

Fostering Self-Compassion: As we revise goals, it's essential to approach ourselves with kindness and self-compassion. Acknowledge that aspirations can evolve, circumstances can change, and the revision process is a natural and healthy aspect of the growth journey.

Strategies for Effective Revision

When the need for goal revision becomes apparent, having a structured approach enhances the effectiveness of the process. Consider the following strategies to guide the revision of goals and affirmations:

Reflect on Current Realities: Begin by reflecting on your current realities—both internal and external. What has changed since you initially set the goal? How do your current circumstances, values, and priorities align with the goal in its current form?

Assess Achievements and Setbacks: Evaluate the progress made toward the goal. What achievements have been celebrated, and what setbacks have been encountered? Understanding the factors influencing progress provides insights into the necessary adjustments.

Clarify Values and Priorities: Revisit your core values and priorities. How do they align with the existing goals? If there has been a shift in values or a reprioritization of aspects in your life, consider how the goals can be adjusted to reflect these changes.

Seek Feedback and Perspectives: Engage in conversations with mentors, accountability partners, or individuals whose perspectives you value. External feedback can provide fresh insights and alternative viewpoints that enrich the revision process.

Break Down Complex Goals: If a goal seems overwhelming or unattainable in its current form, consider breaking it down into smaller, more manageable components. Each component can be reassessed and adjusted, contributing to the overall revision of the overarching goal.

Explore New Avenues: The revision process is an opportune time to explore new avenues or approaches to achieving your aspirations. Are there alternative paths that align better with your current circumstances or offer a more feasible route to your desired outcome?

Set SMART Revisions: Apply the SMART criteria (Specific, Measurable, Achievable, Relevant, and Time-bound) to the revised goals. This ensures that the goals remain clear, actionable, and aligned with the principles of effective goal-setting.

The Role of Flexibility in Goal Setting

Flexibility is the linchpin that holds together the intricate tapestry of goal-setting. The ability to adapt, adjust, and recalibrate goals in response to changing circumstances is an inherent strength on the journey of personal development. Flexibility is not a compromise of commitment but an enhancement—an acknowledgment that the path to growth is a dynamic, ever-shifting terrain.

Adapting to Changing Circumstances: Life is replete with unforeseen events, opportunities, and challenges. The flexibility to adapt goals in response to changing circumstances enables us to navigate the unpredictability of life while staying true to our overarching vision.

Embracing Iterative Progress: Goal-setting is an iterative process, not a linear one. The revision of goals is an integral part of the iterative cycle, allowing for continuous refinement and improvement. Each revision is a step forward in the ongoing journey of personal growth.

Navigating Uncertainty with Grace: The future is inherently uncertain, and the ability to navigate uncertainty with grace is a testament to resilience. Flexibility in goal-setting is a dynamic dance with the unknown, a willingness to adjust our sails as we navigate the seas of transformation.

Aligning with Intrinsic Motivation: Flexibility enables us to align our goals with our intrinsic motivation. As our understanding of ourselves deepens and our authentic desires come to the forefront, the flexibility to revise goals ensures that our aspirations remain authentic and personally meaningful.

Case Studies in Goal Revision

To illustrate the diverse scenarios in which goal revision becomes essential, let's explore case studies featuring individuals who navigated the process of adjusting their goals with flexibility and adaptability.

Case Study 1: Career Pivot

Original Goal: "Become a senior manager in my current department within two years."

Revised Goal: "Explore opportunities for a career pivot, potentially shifting to a different department or industry within the next 18 months."

Reasons for Revision:

- Changed Circumstances: A restructuring in the organization altered the senior management landscape.

- Evolving Priorities: The individual's priorities shifted towards exploring new challenges and opportunities.

- External Feedback: Mentors and colleagues provided insights suggesting a broader range of potential career paths.

Outcome: The individual successfully navigated a career pivot, leveraging transferable skills and exploring new avenues aligned with personal and professional growth. The revised goal not only accommodated changed circumstances but also embraced the evolving aspirations and priorities.

Case Study 2: Health and Wellness

Original Goal: "Lose 20 pounds in three months through a strict diet and exercise regimen."

Revised Goal: "Prioritize overall well-being by adopting a sustainable and balanced approach to nutrition and fitness, aiming for gradual and steady progress."

Reasons for Revision:

- Unrealistic Expectations: The initial goal set an aggressive timeline that proved unsustainable.

- Emotional Disconnect: The strict regimen led to a diminished sense of enjoyment and motivation.

- Learning from Setbacks: Initial setbacks provided insights into the need for a more balanced and realistic approach.

Outcome: By revising the goal to focus on overall well-being and adopting a sustainable approach, the individual experienced a more positive and enjoyable journey. The emphasis shifted from rapid weight loss to long-term health, leading to more lasting and fulfilling results.

Overcoming Challenges in Goal Revision

While the revision of goals is a constructive and necessary aspect of personal development, challenges may arise in the process. Addressing these challenges with a proactive mindset contributes to a smoother and more effective revision process.

Challenge: Fear of Failure or Judgment Strategy: Reframe the perception of revision as a natural part of growth. Emphasize the learning opportunities and positive outcomes that can result from adjusting goals. Seek support from mentors or accountability partners who understand the value of adaptation.

Challenge: Attachment to Original Goals Strategy: Cultivate a mindset of detachment and openness. Recognize that goals are dynamic and subject to change. Focus on the overarching vision and purpose behind the goals, allowing for flexibility in the specific pathways toward achievement.

Challenge: Overemphasis on External Expectations Strategy: Clarify personal values and priorities to ensure that goal-setting aligns with intrinsic motivation. Shift the focus from external expectations to authentic desires and aspirations. Seek feedback from supportive individuals who prioritize individual growth over external benchmarks.

Challenge: Uncertainty and Ambiguity Strategy: Embrace uncertainty as a natural part of the growth journey.

Recognize that ambiguity provides room for exploration and discovery. Break down goals into smaller, manageable steps, focusing on the immediate actions that can be taken.

Conclusion: The Art of Iterative Progress

In the symphony of self-transformation, the art of iterative progress is composed of the dynamic interplay between setting goals, revising them when necessary, and embracing flexibility on the journey. As we navigate the chapters that follow, let the stories of goal revision inspire and empower. Each revision is not a detour but a purposeful step, a calibration that brings us closer to our authentic selves.

May the process of goal revision be a testament to your commitment to growth, a celebration of adaptability, and a recognition that the path to becoming your best self is a nuanced and evolving masterpiece. Together, let us continue to dance with the rhythms of aspiration and adjustment, crafting a symphony of iterative progress in the pursuit of our envisioned future selves.

Chapter 2: Cultivating Gratitude
Research on Benefits

In the tapestry of human emotions, gratitude emerges as a profound and transformative thread, weaving its way through the fabric of our experiences. As we embark on the exploration of cultivating gratitude, it is essential to delve into the rich landscape of scientific research that illuminates the myriad benefits bestowed upon those who embrace this practice. From psychological well-being to physical health, the empirical evidence underscores gratitude as a powerful catalyst for holistic flourishing.

Gratitude Defined: A Scientific Perspective

Before delving into the extensive research on the benefits of gratitude, it's vital to understand how gratitude is defined within the realm of scientific inquiry. Gratitude is more than a fleeting emotion or polite expression of thanks; it is a multifaceted construct encompassing cognitive, emotional, and behavioral elements.

Cognitive Component: Gratitude involves the recognition and acknowledgment of the positive aspects of life. It is the capacity to identify and appreciate the good, whether in people, experiences, or circumstances.

Emotional Component: Emotionally, gratitude encompasses the positive feelings that arise from acknowledging the goodness in one's life. It involves a genuine sense of warmth, joy, and appreciation for the blessings, both big and small.

Behavioral Component: The behavioral aspect of gratitude involves expressing appreciation and reciprocating kindness. Acts of gratitude can take various forms, from verbal expressions of thanks to intentional acts of kindness toward others.

Understanding gratitude in this nuanced way allows researchers to explore its effects comprehensively, encompassing cognitive processes, emotional states, and observable behaviors.

Positive Psychology and Gratitude

Positive psychology, a field that focuses on the study of human strengths and flourishing, has played a pivotal role in illuminating the significance of gratitude. Researchers within positive psychology have conducted numerous studies examining the impact of gratitude on overall well-being, mental health, and interpersonal relationships.

Increased Happiness and Life Satisfaction: Research consistently demonstrates a positive correlation between gratitude and subjective well-being. Grateful individuals tend to report higher levels of happiness and life satisfaction. Multiple studies, including those employing longitudinal designs, have affirmed the enduring nature of this relationship.

Reduced Symptoms of Depression and Anxiety: Gratitude has shown promise as a protective factor against symptoms of depression and anxiety. Individuals who engage in regular gratitude practices, such as keeping a gratitude journal or expressing thanks, often exhibit lower levels of depressive symptoms and anxiety.

Enhanced Positive Affect: Gratitude interventions, such as gratitude journaling, have been linked to increased positive affect. Participants in experimental studies have reported experiencing higher levels of positive emotions after engaging in gratitude-focused activities.

Improved Psychological Well-Being: Beyond the reduction of negative symptoms, gratitude is associated with overall psychological well-being. Studies have explored its connection to facets such as self-esteem, purpose in life, and feelings of autonomy—all contributing to a comprehensive sense of thriving.

Physiological and Neurological Impacts

The benefits of gratitude extend beyond psychological well-being, influencing physiological and neurological processes. Advancements in neuroscientific research have provided insights into the ways gratitude shapes the brain and impacts the body.

Neurological Changes in the Brain: Neuroimaging studies have revealed that practicing gratitude is associated with changes in brain activity, particularly in areas linked to emotional processing and reward. The brain's limbic system, including the amygdala and the ventral striatum, shows increased activation during gratitude-related tasks.

Dopaminergic Pathways and Reward Processing: Gratitude is intricately connected to the brain's reward system, which relies on the neurotransmitter dopamine. When individuals experience and express gratitude, the brain's dopaminergic pathways are activated, reinforcing positive behaviors and motivating continued expressions of thanks.

Reduction in Stress and Inflammation: Chronic stress and inflammation are significant contributors to various health issues. Studies have suggested that gratitude practices may mitigate the impact of stress on the body, leading to reductions in markers of inflammation. The cultivation of positive emotions, including gratitude, appears to exert a protective effect on physiological well-being.

Enhanced Sleep Quality: Gratitude interventions have been linked to improvements in sleep quality. Expressing gratitude before bedtime and focusing on positive aspects of the day contribute to a more positive mindset, potentially facilitating better sleep patterns.

Impact on Interpersonal Relationships

Gratitude has a profound impact on the quality of interpersonal relationships, fostering connection, and fortifying the social fabric. Research in this domain explores how gratitude influences relationship dynamics, communication, and the overall health of social connections.

Strengthening Social Bonds: Gratitude serves as a relational glue, strengthening social bonds and creating a sense of connection between individuals. Expressions of gratitude contribute to a positive feedback loop, reinforcing prosocial behaviors and enhancing the quality of relationships.

Conflict Resolution and Forgiveness: In the context of relationships, gratitude has been linked to effective conflict resolution and forgiveness. Grateful individuals may approach conflicts with a more positive and constructive mindset, facilitating resolution and the ability to forgive transgressions.

Altruistic Behavior and Cooperation: Gratitude is associated with an increased likelihood of engaging in altruistic behaviors and cooperative actions. Individuals who experience and express gratitude are more inclined to contribute to the well-being of others, fostering a sense of communal support.

Enhanced Communication and Empathy: Grateful individuals tend to exhibit enhanced communication skills and empathy. The practice of gratitude encourages active listening, authentic expression of appreciation, and a heightened awareness of others' emotions.

Gratitude and Physical Health

The mind-body connection becomes evident in the intersection of gratitude and physical health. Research has uncovered intriguing associations between gratitude practices and various markers of physical well-being.

Cardiovascular Health: Preliminary studies suggest that gratitude may have cardiovascular benefits. Grateful individuals have been found to engage in heart-healthy behaviors, such as regular exercise and a balanced diet, contributing to overall cardiovascular well-being.

Immune System Function: Gratitude practices have been associated with positive effects on immune system function. The cultivation of positive emotions, including gratitude, may have immunomodulatory effects, enhancing the body's ability to defend against illness.

Pain Perception and Coping: For individuals dealing with chronic pain or health challenges, gratitude has shown promise in influencing pain perception and coping mechanisms. Gratitude interventions have been explored as complementary approaches in pain management.

Longevity and Aging Well: While the field is still emerging, some studies suggest a potential link between gratitude and longevity. The positive impact of gratitude on mental and emotional well-being may contribute to aging well and experiencing a higher quality of life in later years.

Cultivating Gratitude: Practical Applications

As the research on gratitude continues to unfold, practical applications emerge, offering individuals tangible ways to incorporate gratitude into their daily lives. The following strategies, inspired by scientific findings, provide actionable steps for cultivating gratitude:

Gratitude Journaling: Regularly journaling about things for which one is thankful has been a widely studied and effective gratitude practice. Setting aside time each day or week to reflect on positive experiences and express gratitude in writing reinforces the cognitive and emotional components of gratitude.

Expressing Gratitude to Others: Actively expressing gratitude to others—whether through verbal acknowledgment, handwritten notes, or acts of kindness—contributes to the behavioral aspect of gratitude. These expressions not only benefit the recipient but also enhance the well-being of the giver.

Mindful Gratitude Practices: Incorporating mindfulness into gratitude practices amplifies their impact. Mindful gratitude involves being fully present and savoring the positive aspects of the present moment. Mindfulness enhances the depth of emotional experiences associated with gratitude.

Gratitude Letters and Visits: Writing letters expressing gratitude to individuals who have positively impacted one's life and, in some cases, delivering these letters in person, has been shown to have lasting positive effects on well-being. This practice deepens social connections and fosters a sense of appreciation.

Gratitude in the Workplace: Extending gratitude practices to the workplace enhances job satisfaction, teamwork, and overall organizational climate. Employers and employees alike can benefit from incorporating gratitude into the workplace culture, whether through formal recognition programs or informal expressions of thanks.

Overcoming Challenges in Cultivating Gratitude

While the benefits of cultivating gratitude are well-established, individuals may encounter challenges in integrating gratitude practices into their lives. Understanding and addressing these challenges is integral to creating sustainable and meaningful gratitude habits.

Challenge: Perceived Lack of Time Strategy: Integrate gratitude practices into existing routines. Whether during morning or evening rituals, find pockets of time for gratitude journaling, reflection, or expressions of thanks. Small, consistent efforts can yield significant benefits.

Challenge: Difficulty in Finding Things to Be Grateful For Strategy: Expand the scope of gratitude beyond major events. Focus on small, everyday blessings and moments of joy. Cultivate an awareness of the ordinary wonders that often go unnoticed, such as a beautiful sunrise, a kind gesture, or a moment of laughter.

Challenge: Overcoming Negativity Bias Strategy: Counteract the brain's natural tendency toward negativity bias by intentionally seeking out positive aspects of experiences. Actively redirect attention toward positive elements, even in challenging situations, to cultivate a more balanced perspective.

Challenge: Maintaining Consistency Strategy: Start with manageable goals and gradually increase the frequency and depth of gratitude practices. Consistency is key, and establishing a routine that aligns with personal preferences and lifestyle increases the likelihood of sustained engagement.

Conclusion: Gratitude as a Path to Flourishing

As we navigate the vast landscape of gratitude research, one overarching truth becomes evident: gratitude is not merely a fleeting emotion or polite gesture; it is a pathway to flourishing. From the realms of positive psychology to the intricacies of neural pathways, the evidence is compelling—cultivating gratitude has far-reaching benefits for the mind, body, and soul.

As we proceed to the subsequent chapters, let the wisdom of research guide our exploration of gratitude practices. From the cognitive dimensions of recognizing the good to the physiological impacts on health, each aspect contributes to a holistic understanding of gratitude as a transformative force. Let the research serve as a beacon, illuminating the path toward a life enriched by the practice of gratitude—a life where the simple act of giving thanks becomes a profound journey of self-discovery and well-being.

Morning Reflection Rituals

In the symphony of daily life, the morning represents a powerful overture—a harmonious prelude that sets the tone for the day ahead. Within the realm of cultivating gratitude, morning reflection rituals emerge as a poignant and transformative practice. As the first rays of sunlight illuminate the canvas of a new day, these rituals invite individuals to intentionally cultivate gratitude, infusing each waking moment with a sense of appreciation and mindfulness. In this exploration, we delve into the art and science of morning reflection rituals, uncovering their profound impact on mental well-being, emotional resilience, and the overall tapestry of a flourishing life.

The Essence of Morning Reflection

At its core, morning reflection is a deliberate and conscious practice that invites individuals to engage in introspection, gratitude, and mindfulness at the beginning of each day. Unlike the hurried pace that often characterizes mornings, reflection rituals create a sacred space for individuals to connect with themselves, their surroundings, and the possibilities that lie ahead. While the specific elements of morning reflection may vary based on personal preferences, cultural influences, or spiritual beliefs, the essence remains rooted in the intentional cultivation of a positive and grateful mindset.

The Science Behind Morning Reflection

Before delving into the practical aspects of morning reflection rituals, it's insightful to explore the scientific foundations that underscore their efficacy. Research in positive psychology and neuroscience provides valuable insights into how morning reflection rituals influence cognitive processes, emotional states, and overall well-being.

Cognitive Priming: Morning reflection serves as a form of cognitive priming, shaping the way individuals perceive and interpret events throughout the day. By consciously focusing on positive aspects, individuals set a positive cognitive bias that influences their attention and interpretation of subsequent experiences.

Neuroplasticity and Habit Formation: The morning hours are particularly conducive to habit formation due to the brain's heightened neuroplasticity during this time. Engaging in morning reflection consistently establishes neural pathways associated with gratitude and positive thinking, making these practices more automatic over time.

Cortisol Regulation: Morning reflection has been linked to cortisol regulation, the hormone associated with stress. By incorporating calming and gratitude-focused activities, individuals may modulate cortisol levels, contributing to a more balanced and resilient stress response.

Positive Emotion Activation: Morning reflection rituals activate neural circuits associated with positive emotions, including the release of neurotransmitters such as dopamine and serotonin. This neurochemical cascade sets a positive emotional tone for the day, influencing mood, motivation, and resilience.

Elements of Morning Reflection Rituals

Morning reflection rituals encompass a diverse array of practices that cater to individual preferences and resonate with personal values. While the specific elements may vary, the following components exemplify the essence of morning reflection:

Gratitude Journaling: Writing down three things for which one is grateful is a simple yet potent practice. Whether in a physical journal or a digital platform, the act of articulating gratitude anchors positive emotions and creates a tangible record of blessings.

Mindful Breathing Exercises: Incorporating mindful breathing exercises into morning reflection cultivates a sense of calm and presence. Techniques such as deep diaphragmatic breathing or mindful breath awareness center individuals in the present moment.

Visualization: Engaging in positive visualization involves mentally picturing one's goals, aspirations, or desired outcomes. Visualizing a successful and fulfilling day ahead sets a positive trajectory for the mind.

Affirmations: Reciting affirmations that align with personal values and aspirations reinforces positive beliefs. Affirmations serve as powerful self-talk, influencing mindset and self-perception.

Expressing Intentions: Setting clear intentions for the day provides a sense of purpose and direction. Whether through written statements or spoken affirmations, expressing intentions guides actions and choices throughout the day.

Gratitude Letters or Notes: Taking a few moments to write a note of gratitude to oneself or expressing appreciation for someone else creates a positive and reciprocal energy. These notes can be revisited throughout the day as reminders of gratitude.

Connecting with Nature: Spending time in nature, whether through a brief walk, gazing at the sunrise, or simply appreciating natural elements, fosters a sense of connection and grounding.

Mindful Movement: Incorporating gentle movements or stretches, such as yoga or tai chi, into morning reflection rituals enhances physical well-being and promotes a mind-body connection.

Practical Applications: Designing Your Morning Reflection Ritual

Creating a personalized morning reflection ritual involves a thoughtful blend of practices that resonate with individual preferences and lifestyle. The following guidelines offer a framework for designing a morning reflection ritual that aligns with personal needs and goals:

Start with Intention: Begin the morning reflection ritual with a clear intention. Reflect on the purpose of the ritual—whether it's to cultivate gratitude, set a positive tone, or create a moment of mindfulness. Clarifying intention provides a guiding focus.

Create a Sacred Space: Designate a physical or mental space for morning reflection. This space should evoke a sense of tranquility and mindfulness. It could be a quiet corner, a favorite chair, or simply the mental space cultivated through intentional focus.

Set Realistic Duration: Consider the available time in the morning routine and set a realistic duration for the reflection ritual. While even a few minutes can be impactful, it's essential to choose a duration that fits seamlessly into the morning routine.

Choose Practices Mindfully: Select practices that resonate with personal preferences and goals. Whether it's gratitude journaling, mindful breathing, or visualization, each practice should contribute to a positive and meaningful start to the day.

Adapt and Evolve: Recognize that morning reflection rituals can evolve over time. As personal preferences change, goals shift, or circumstances vary, be open to adapting the ritual to align with the current needs and aspirations.

Case Studies: Morning Reflection in Action

To illustrate the diverse ways individuals incorporate morning reflection rituals into their lives, let's explore case studies featuring individuals who have experienced transformative outcomes through intentional morning practices.

Case Study 1: Sarah's Gratitude Journaling

Background: Sarah, a marketing professional with a demanding schedule, struggled with stress and feelings of overwhelm.

Morning Reflection Ritual: Sarah introduced gratitude journaling into her morning routine. Each day, she dedicated five minutes to write down three things she was grateful for, focusing on specific moments or aspects of her life.

Outcomes:

- Reduced Stress Levels: Over time, Sarah noticed a significant reduction in her stress levels. The act of reflecting on positive aspects of her life each morning created a buffer against daily stressors.

- Increased Positivity: Gratitude journaling contributed to a more positive mindset. Sarah found herself approaching challenges with a greater sense of resilience and optimism.

- Enhanced Well-Being: The ritual became a source of emotional well-being, providing a daily anchor of positivity that influenced her overall mood and interactions throughout the day.

Case Study 2: David's Mindful Movement Practice

Background: David, a software engineer, experienced challenges with focus and work-related stress.

Morning Reflection Ritual: David incorporated mindful movement, specifically a series of yoga stretches and breathing exercises, into his morning routine. He dedicated 15 minutes to these practices each morning.

Outcomes:

- Improved Focus and Concentration: The mindful movement practices helped David enhance his focus and concentration. The combination of gentle stretches and controlled breathing acted as a mental reset, preparing him for the workday.

- Reduced Physical Tension: David experienced a reduction in physical tension and discomfort associated with sitting at a desk for long periods. The morning stretches contributed to improved posture and physical well-being.

- Enhanced Mind-Body Connection: The intentional focus on breath and movement fostered a greater awareness of the mind-body connection. David felt more attuned to his body's signals and needs throughout the day.

Overcoming Challenges in Morning Reflection

While morning reflection rituals offer numerous benefits, individuals may encounter challenges in establishing and maintaining these practices. Addressing common challenges enhances the likelihood of sustained engagement:

Challenge: Inconsistent Schedule Strategy: Design a flexible reflection ritual that can be adapted to varying schedules. Identify core elements that can be consistently incorporated, even during busy mornings. Consistency is more important than duration.

Challenge: Morning Fatigue Strategy: Start with brief practices that are invigorating rather than draining. Incorporate practices that engage the body and mind, such as gentle stretches or a few minutes of deep breathing. Gradually increase the duration as energy levels permit.

Challenge: Resistance to Change Strategy: Introduce morning reflection gradually, incorporating one or two practices at a time. Allow time to adjust and recognize the positive effects. Frame the ritual as an opportunity for self-care rather than an additional task.

Challenge: Overwhelming Options Strategy: Begin with a small set of practices and gradually experiment with additional elements. Choose practices that align with personal preferences and resonate with individual goals. The key is to create a ritual that feels authentic and sustainable.

Conclusion: Embracing the Dawn of Transformation

As we navigate the realms of morning reflection rituals, let the dawn of each day become a canvas for intentional and transformative practices. From the tranquility of gratitude journaling to the mindful cadence of movement, morning reflection rituals offer a portal to self-discovery, well-being, and the art of starting each day with purpose.

May the exploration of morning reflection rituals inspire a sense of curiosity and a commitment to weaving intentional moments into the tapestry of daily life. As we venture into the subsequent chapters, let the essence of morning reflection linger—an invitation to embrace the dawn of each day as an opportunity for gratitude, mindfulness, and the unfolding journey of self-transformation.

Gratitude Journaling

In the kaleidoscope of human experiences, gratitude journaling emerges as a powerful and accessible practice—a transformative act of introspection that invites individuals to consciously acknowledge and appreciate the positive aspects of their lives. Within the tapestry of morning reflection rituals, gratitude journaling holds a special place, offering a tangible and enduring record of blessings, big and small. In this exploration, we delve into the art and science of gratitude journaling, uncovering its profound impact on mental well-being, emotional resilience, and the cultivation of a grateful mindset.

The Essence of Gratitude Journaling

At its essence, gratitude journaling is a deliberate and reflective practice that involves regularly recording moments, experiences, or aspects of life for which one is grateful. Whether expressed through words, images, or a combination of both, the act of journaling serves as a conduit for acknowledging and amplifying the positive elements that often go unnoticed in the hustle of daily life. Gratitude journaling is not merely a documentation of events; it is a conscious cultivation of gratitude—a process that unfolds the petals of appreciation, fostering a deep connection with the present moment.

The Science Behind Gratitude Journaling

Before delving into the practical aspects of gratitude journaling, it's illuminating to explore the scientific underpinnings that underscore its efficacy. Research in positive psychology, neuroscience, and behavioral science provides valuable insights into how gratitude journaling influences cognitive processes, emotional states, and overall well-being.

Cognitive Restructuring: Gratitude journaling operates as a form of cognitive restructuring—a process that involves reframing and shifting cognitive patterns. By consciously focusing on positive elements, individuals engage in a form of selective attention, directing their awareness toward the good rather than fixating on the negative.

Neuroplasticity and Positive Habits: The consistent practice of gratitude journaling leverages the brain's neuroplasticity—the ability to reorganize and form new neural connections. Over time, this practice establishes positive habits of thought, creating neural pathways associated with gratitude and a positive mindset.

Emotional Regulation: Gratitude journaling contributes to emotional regulation by enhancing emotional intelligence and awareness. The act of identifying and articulating positive emotions fosters emotional clarity and resilience, providing a buffer against stress and negative emotions.

Positive Reinforcement: The act of writing down moments of gratitude reinforces positive experiences. The physical act of recording these moments serves as a tangible reminder, creating a positive feedback loop that reinforces the likelihood of noticing and appreciating positive elements in the future.

The Art of Gratitude Journaling

Gratitude journaling is a flexible and personal practice that can take various forms, adapting to individual preferences and styles. While there is no one-size-fits-all approach, several key elements characterize the art of gratitude journaling:

Regular Practice: Consistency is foundational to the efficacy of gratitude journaling. Whether daily, weekly, or at another frequency that aligns with individual routines, the key is to establish a regular practice that becomes an integral part of the daily or weekly rhythm.

Specificity and Detail: The richness of gratitude journaling lies in the specificity and detail of the entries. Instead of generic statements, individuals are encouraged to delve into the particulars of what they are grateful for—specific experiences, actions, or qualities that evoke a sense of appreciation.

Variety of Entries: Gratitude journaling extends beyond conventional written entries. While written expressions are common, individuals can explore a variety of mediums, including drawing, collage, or multimedia formats. The diversity of expressions allows for a more holistic engagement with gratitude.

Reflection and Intentions: Integrating reflection and intentions amplifies the impact of gratitude journaling. Alongside recording moments of gratitude, individuals can reflect on the emotions associated with these moments and set intentions for fostering gratitude in the future.

Flexibility and Adaptability: Gratitude journaling is a dynamic practice that evolves with the individual. As circumstances, priorities, and emotional landscapes shift, the practice can adapt. Flexibility in the approach ensures that gratitude journaling remains a source of inspiration rather than a rigid task.

Practical Applications: Initiating Gratitude Journaling

Embarking on the journey of gratitude journaling involves a thoughtful and intentional approach. The following guidelines provide a framework for initiating and sustaining a gratitude journaling practice:

Select a Journal: Choose a journal or platform that resonates with personal preferences. Whether a traditional notebook, a digital app, or a multimedia format, the selected journal should feel inviting and aligned with individual style.

Set Aside Dedicated Time: Designate a specific time for gratitude journaling that integrates seamlessly into the daily or weekly routine. Whether in the morning, before bedtime, or during breaks, consistency in timing establishes a ritualistic aspect of the practice.

Start Small: Begin with manageable goals, especially if new to the practice. Setting the bar too high can lead to overwhelm. Start with a commitment to journaling a few times a week or even once a week, gradually increasing frequency as the practice becomes more ingrained.

Focus on the Present: While reflecting on past experiences is valuable, emphasize the present moment in gratitude journaling. Direct attention to current blessings and positive aspects of the immediate environment to foster a sense of immediacy and mindfulness.

Experiment with Formats: Explore different formats of gratitude journaling. Beyond written entries, consider incorporating visual elements, such as drawings, photographs, or collages. The variety of formats adds a creative dimension to the practice.

Case Studies: Transformative Journeys Through Gratitude Journaling

To illustrate the diverse ways individuals have experienced transformative outcomes through gratitude journaling, let's explore case studies featuring individuals who embarked on this intentional practice.

Case Study 1: Emily's Daily Gratitude Ritual

Background: Emily, a college student dealing with academic stress and anxiety, sought a way to cultivate a more positive mindset.

Gratitude Journaling Practice: Emily initiated a daily gratitude ritual, dedicating a few minutes each evening to reflect on three things she was grateful for that day. She recorded these moments in a dedicated gratitude journal.

Outcomes:

- Stress Reduction: Emily experienced a notable reduction in stress levels. The practice of focusing on positive moments served as a counterbalance to the academic pressures she faced.

- Improved Mood: The daily gratitude ritual contributed to an improved mood. Emily found herself approaching challenges with a more optimistic mindset, fostering a greater sense of emotional well-being.

- Enhanced Perspective: Gratitude journaling helped Emily gain perspective on the positive elements in her life. The practice became a source of resilience, providing a daily reminder of the good amid academic demands.

Case Study 2: James' Visual Gratitude Collage

Background: James, a professional dealing with the demands of a high-pressure job, sought a creative and visual approach to gratitude.

Gratitude Journaling Practice: James created a visual gratitude collage as his journaling format. Using a combination of images, magazine cutouts, and his own drawings, he visually represented moments of gratitude.

Outcomes:

- Enhanced Creativity: James found the visual format to be a creative outlet. The act of visually representing moments of gratitude allowed him to express his emotions in a way that words alone couldn't capture.

- Daily Reflection: The process of creating the collage became a form of daily reflection. James spent a few minutes each evening selecting images and arranging them, fostering a contemplative and intentional mindset.

- Tangible Reminder: The visual gratitude collage served as a tangible reminder of positive experiences. Placed in a visible location, it became a touchstone throughout the day, reinforcing a positive and grateful orientation.

Overcoming Challenges in Gratitude Journaling

While gratitude journaling holds immense potential for positive transformation, individuals may encounter challenges along the way. Addressing these challenges enhances the sustainability and meaningfulness of the practice:

Challenge: Perceived Lack of Time Strategy: Start with brief entries that can be completed in a few minutes. Gratitude journaling doesn't require extensive time commitments. Even a brief reflection can yield significant benefits.

Challenge: Difficulty Identifying Blessings Strategy: Expand the definition of gratitude to include small, everyday blessings. Instead of focusing solely on major events, pay attention to moments of beauty, kindness, or joy that may go unnoticed.

Challenge: Fear of Monotony Strategy: Introduce variety into the practice by experimenting with different formats, such as visual expressions, poetry, or themed entries. Variety prevents the practice from becoming monotonous and enhances creativity.

Challenge: Unfulfilled Expectations Strategy: Adjust expectations and embrace the evolving nature of the practice. Gratitude journaling is a journey, and the benefits may unfold gradually. Celebrate small victories and moments of joy along the way.

Conclusion: The Alchemy of Gratitude Journaling

As we explore the alchemy of gratitude journaling, let the blank pages of the journal become a canvas for the art of appreciation. From the ink of written words to the hues of visual expressions, gratitude journaling offers a space to document the beauty and blessings that color the canvas of our lives.

May the practice of gratitude journaling become a cherished ritual—an intentional journey of self-discovery, resilience, and the cultivation of a grateful heart. As we transition to the subsequent chapters, let the essence of gratitude journaling linger—a testament to the transformative power of acknowledging and celebrating the abundance that resides in the ordinary and extraordinary moments of life.

Unexpected Blessings

In the intricate dance of life, there exists a profound beauty in the unexpected—a serendipitous symphony of moments that defy prediction and offer glimpses into the extraordinary. Within the realm of gratitude cultivation, the practice of acknowledging and embracing unexpected blessings stands as a beacon of appreciation for the unforeseen gifts that grace our lives. In this exploration, we embark on a journey into the heart of unexpected blessings, unraveling the art and science of recognizing, savoring, and expressing gratitude for the delightful surprises that often go unnoticed.

The Essence of Unexpected Blessings

Unexpected blessings, often referred to as serendipity or fortuitous events, are those delightful surprises that catch us off guard, evoking a sense of joy, wonder, or gratitude. These blessings may manifest as chance encounters, unforeseen opportunities, or moments of beauty that unfold without anticipation. The essence of unexpected blessings lies in their ability to transcend the boundaries of routine, injecting a dose of magic into the fabric of everyday life.

The Science Behind Recognizing Unexpected Blessings

Before delving into the practical aspects of acknowledging unexpected blessings, it's insightful to explore the scientific foundations that underpin our ability to recognize and appreciate these serendipitous moments. Research in positive psychology and cognitive science provides valuable insights into the mechanisms that shape our perception of unexpected blessings.

Cognitive Flexibility: Cognitive flexibility, the ability to adapt thinking to new and unexpected information, plays a pivotal role in recognizing unexpected blessings. Individuals with higher cognitive flexibility are more adept at shifting their attention and interpretations, allowing them to notice and appreciate unexpected positive events.

Positive Psychology and Resilience: The field of positive psychology highlights the importance of resilience—the capacity to bounce back from adversity. Recognizing and savoring unexpected blessings contributes to resilience by fostering a positive mindset even in the face of challenges. Resilient individuals are more likely to perceive and capitalize on unexpected positive events.

Mindfulness and Presence: Mindfulness, the practice of being fully present in the moment, enhances our capacity to notice and savor unexpected blessings. By cultivating a state of mindfulness, individuals become more attuned to their surroundings, relationships, and the subtle nuances of life, increasing the likelihood of recognizing serendipitous moments.

Neurotransmitters and Reward Systems: The brain's reward system, governed by neurotransmitters such as dopamine, plays a role in the perception of unexpected rewards. When individuals encounter a positive surprise, the brain releases dopamine, reinforcing the behavior of noticing and appreciating unexpected blessings.

Savoring the Unforeseen: A Practical Guide

Savoring unexpected blessings involves a deliberate and mindful approach to acknowledging and appreciating the positive surprises that unfold in our lives. The following elements contribute to the art of savoring the unforeseen:

Cultivating Awareness: The first step in savoring unexpected blessings is cultivating awareness. This involves developing a heightened sensitivity to the present moment, actively engaging the senses, and being attuned to the potential for positive surprises.

Mindful Presence: Practicing mindfulness is a key component of savoring unexpected blessings. By being fully present in the moment, individuals create the mental space to notice and absorb the richness of positive surprises, whether they are small delights or significant events.

Gratitude Journaling for Serendipity: Incorporating unexpected blessings into gratitude journaling deepens the practice. When unexpected positive events occur, taking a moment to jot them down in a gratitude journal magnifies their impact and creates a lasting record of joy.

Sharing Joy with Others: The act of sharing unexpected blessings with others amplifies the joy experienced. Whether through verbal expressions, sharing the story, or engaging in acts of kindness inspired by the positive surprise, spreading joy contributes to a communal sense of well-being.

Creating Space for Serendipity: Intentionally creating space for serendipity involves cultivating an openness to the unexpected. This might include stepping outside of comfort zones, embracing spontaneity, and relinquishing rigid expectations to allow room for positive surprises to unfold.

Case Studies: Embracing the Magic of Unexpected Blessings

To illustrate the transformative power of acknowledging and savoring unexpected blessings, let's explore case studies featuring individuals who have embraced the magic of serendipity in their lives.

Case Study 1: Maria's Chance Encounter

Background: Maria, a graphic designer navigating a period of creative block, sought inspiration and a renewed sense of purpose.

Unexpected Blessing: While taking a break at a local coffee shop, Maria struck up a conversation with a stranger who happened to be a renowned artist. This chance encounter led to a mentorship, reigniting Maria's passion for design.

Outcomes:

- Creative Renewal: The unexpected meeting served as a catalyst for Maria's creative renewal. The mentorship provided fresh perspectives, new techniques, and a renewed sense of purpose in her artistic endeavors.

- Expanded Networks: The chance encounter expanded Maria's professional networks. The mentorship not only provided guidance in her creative pursuits but also opened doors to collaborations and opportunities within the artistic community.

- Enhanced Well-Being: Embracing the unexpected blessing had a positive impact on Maria's overall well-being. The sense of connection, inspiration, and renewed passion contributed to a more fulfilling and joyful life.

Case Study 2: Jonathan's Serendipitous Job Offer

Background: Jonathan, an IT professional, was contemplating a career change but was unsure about taking the leap.

Unexpected Blessing: While attending a local tech event, Jonathan struck up a conversation with a participant who turned out to be the CEO of a company in his desired industry. This chance meeting led to a job offer that aligned with his aspirations.

Outcomes:

- Career Alignment: The unexpected job offer aligned perfectly with Jonathan's career aspirations. It provided an opportunity to transition into a new industry and take on a role that resonated with his long-term goals.

- Personal Growth: Embracing the unexpected blessing prompted personal growth. Jonathan stepped out of his comfort zone, navigated a career transition, and gained valuable experiences that contributed to his professional and personal development.

- Increased Confidence: Successfully navigating the career change bolstered Jonathan's confidence. The serendipitous job offer became a pivotal moment that instilled a belief in his ability to navigate uncertain situations and make meaningful career choices.

Gratitude in Action: Expressing Thanks for Unexpected Blessings

Expressing gratitude for unexpected blessings involves both acknowledging the positive surprise and conveying appreciation for the joy it brings. The following elements contribute to expressing thanks for unexpected blessings:

Verbal Expressions: Simply expressing gratitude verbally, whether through words of thanks or sharing the joy with others, is a meaningful way to acknowledge and appreciate unexpected blessings.

Acts of Kindness: Paying the positive surprise forward through acts of kindness creates a ripple effect of joy. Whether through a small gesture or a more significant act, spreading kindness contributes to a culture of gratitude.

Reflection and Integration: Taking time to reflect on the impact of the unexpected blessing and integrating its lessons or joy into one's life deepens the gratitude experience. This reflection may involve journaling, meditation, or other contemplative practices.

Creating a Gratitude Ritual: Establishing a gratitude ritual specifically dedicated to unexpected blessings enhances the practice. This ritual might involve a weekly reflection on positive surprises or a special way of expressing thanks, such as writing thank-you notes.

Conclusion: Navigating the Landscape of Serendipity

As we navigate the landscape of unexpected blessings, let the lens of gratitude be our guide. From chance encounters to unforeseen opportunities, unexpected blessings invite us to savor the magic woven into the fabric of our lives.

May the exploration of serendipity inspire a heightened awareness of the extraordinary in the ordinary. As we transition to the subsequent chapters, let the essence of unexpected blessings linger—a reminder to embrace the joy, wonder, and gratitude that arise when we open our hearts to the delightful surprises that grace our journey.

Chapter 3: Practicing Mindfulness
Understanding Autopilot Habits

In the tapestry of daily life, many of our actions unfold seamlessly, guided by the well-worn grooves of habit. These autopilot habits, deeply ingrained patterns of behavior, influence our thoughts, emotions, and responses without conscious awareness. Within the realm of mindfulness, understanding autopilot habits is a pivotal step toward cultivating a heightened awareness of the present moment. In this exploration, we delve into the intricacies of autopilot habits, unraveling their impact on our lives and discovering how mindfulness becomes a transformative tool for breaking free from the unconscious patterns that shape our daily existence.

The Nature of Autopilot Habits

Autopilot habits, also known as automatic or unconscious habits, are behaviors that unfold automatically, without deliberate intention or conscious awareness. These habits are often deeply ingrained through repetition, becoming second nature over time. From the mundane rituals of morning routines to the emotional responses triggered by specific situations, autopilot habits shape a significant portion of our daily experiences.

The Science Behind Autopilot Habits

Understanding the science behind autopilot habits involves exploring the neurological and psychological mechanisms that underpin their formation and perpetuation.

Neuroplasticity: The brain's remarkable capacity for neuroplasticity—the ability to reorganize itself in response to experience—plays a key role in the formation of autopilot habits. Repetitive behaviors create neural pathways that become increasingly efficient, leading to automatic responses.

Habit Loop: The habit loop, a concept proposed by Charles Duhigg in "The Power of Habit," consists of three components: cue, routine, and reward. Autopilot habits follow this loop, where a specific cue triggers a habitual routine that is then rewarded, reinforcing the loop and perpetuating the habit.

Dopamine Reinforcement: The release of dopamine, a neurotransmitter associated with pleasure and reward, reinforces autopilot habits. When the brain anticipates a reward linked to a particular habit, dopamine is released, creating a positive association and reinforcing the habit loop.

Role of Basal Ganglia: The basal ganglia, a group of structures deep within the brain, plays a crucial role in habit formation. As habits become more automatic, the basal ganglia takes over, allowing the behavior to unfold with minimal conscious effort.

Common Autopilot Habits

Autopilot habits manifest in various aspects of our lives, influencing our behaviors, thoughts, and emotional responses. Some common autopilot habits include:

Morning Routine Rituals: The sequence of activities we engage in upon waking often becomes automatic, from the order in which we get ready to the steps of preparing breakfast.

Emotional Reactions: Certain situations or interactions may trigger automatic emotional responses, such as frustration, anxiety, or joy, without conscious consideration.

Procrastination Patterns: Procrastination, a common autopilot habit, involves delaying tasks automatically without a conscious decision to do so.

Thought Patterns: Repetitive thought patterns, such as worrying about the future or dwelling on past events, can become habitual and automatic.

Social Interactions: The way we engage in social interactions, including communication styles and body language, can be influenced by autopilot habits.

The Impact of Autopilot Habits on Well-Being

While autopilot habits serve a purpose by conserving mental energy and facilitating efficiency, they can also have significant implications for well-being when left unchecked.

Mindless Living: Autopilot habits contribute to mindless living, where days unfold without conscious awareness or intention. This mindlessness can lead to a sense of disconnection from experiences and a lack of fulfillment.

Reactivity and Stress: Automatic emotional reactions can contribute to heightened stress levels. Reacting impulsively without conscious consideration may lead to increased emotional volatility and difficulty in managing stress.

Limiting Behavior: Autopilot habits, when unchecked, can contribute to limiting behavior by reinforcing patterns that may not align with personal goals or values. Breaking free from these habits requires a conscious shift in awareness.

Reduced Creativity: Mindless repetition can stifle creativity by limiting the exploration of new perspectives and approaches. Autopilot habits may contribute to a sense of monotony and hinder the discovery of innovative solutions.

The Role of Mindfulness in Breaking Autopilot Habits

Mindfulness, rooted in the practice of being fully present and aware in the current moment, serves as a powerful antidote to autopilot habits. By cultivating mindfulness, individuals gain the ability to observe, understand, and eventually transform their automatic responses. Here are key aspects of how mindfulness facilitates the breaking of autopilot habits:

Awareness of Cues: Mindfulness involves heightened awareness of cues that trigger habitual responses. By recognizing the cues, individuals gain the ability to interrupt the habit loop before the routine unfolds.

Non-Judgmental Observation: Mindfulness encourages non-judgmental observation of thoughts, emotions, and behaviors. Rather than reacting automatically, individuals learn to observe with curiosity and without attaching judgments.

Conscious Choice: Through mindfulness, individuals develop the capacity to make conscious choices rather than succumbing to automatic responses. This involves pausing to reflect on the most intentional and aligned course of action.

Present-Moment Focus: Mindfulness directs attention to the present moment, breaking the cycle of mindless repetition. By fully engaging with the current experience, individuals disrupt the automatic nature of habitual responses.

Cultivation of Response Flexibility: Mindfulness fosters response flexibility—the ability to adapt and choose responses that align with current goals and values. This flexibility is essential for breaking free from rigid autopilot habits.

Practicing Mindfulness to Break Autopilot Habits

Embarking on the journey of breaking autopilot habits through mindfulness involves intentional and consistent practice. Here are practical steps individuals can take:

Mindful Breathing: Begin by incorporating mindful breathing exercises into daily routines. Focus on the breath, observing each inhalation and exhalation with full attention. This practice enhances present-moment awareness.

Body Scan Meditation: The body scan meditation involves directing attention to different parts of the body, cultivating awareness of physical sensations. This practice promotes a connection between mind and body, breaking the automatic nature of habitual responses.

Mindful Observation: Engage in mindful observation of daily activities. Whether eating, walking, or engaging in routine tasks, bring full attention to the sensory experiences and details of the present moment.

Thought Labeling: When automatic thoughts arise, practice thought labeling. Instead of getting entangled in the content of the thoughts, label them with neutral terms such as "thinking" or "planning." This technique creates distance from automatic thought patterns.

Mindful Reflection: Dedicate time for mindful reflection, especially at the end of the day. Review experiences, interactions, and emotional responses with a non-judgmental and curious awareness. Identify instances where autopilot habits may have influenced behavior.

Case Studies: Transformative Journeys Through Mindfulness

To illustrate the transformative power of mindfulness in breaking autopilot habits, let's explore case studies featuring individuals who embarked on this intentional practice.

Case Study 1: Sarah's Mindful Eating Journey

Background: Sarah, a marketing professional, struggled with mindless eating habits and emotional eating as a response to stress.

Mindful Eating Practice:

- Awareness of Triggers: Sarah cultivated awareness of the emotional triggers that led to mindless eating. She identified stress, boredom, and fatigue as common cues for automatic eating.

- Savoring the Eating Experience: During meals, Sarah practiced savoring each bite by paying attention to the flavors, textures, and aromas of the food. This mindfulness allowed her to break the automatic pattern of rapid and distracted eating.

- Conscious Food Choices: Mindful reflection helped Sarah make conscious choices about the foods she consumed. She began to choose nourishing options that aligned with her well-being goals.

Outcomes:

- Emotional Regulation: Mindful eating contributed to better emotional regulation. Sarah developed the ability to sit with and understand her emotions without resorting to automatic eating as a coping mechanism.

- Improved Relationship with Food: The practice of mindful eating transformed Sarah's relationship with food. She began to view meals as opportunities for nourishment and enjoyment rather than as automatic responses to emotions.

- Enhanced Well-Being: Breaking the autopilot habit of mindless eating had a ripple effect on Sarah's overall well-being. She felt more in control of her choices, experienced increased energy levels, and developed a greater sense of mindfulness in other aspects of her life.

Case Study 2: Alex's Mindful Communication Journey

Background: Alex, a project manager, struggled with automatic and reactive communication patterns that often led to misunderstandings with colleagues.

Mindful Communication Practice:

- Pause and Reflect: Alex incorporated a pause before responding to emails, messages, or verbal communication. This intentional pause allowed him to step out of automatic reactions and reflect on the most mindful and effective response.

- Active Listening: During meetings and conversations, Alex practiced active listening. Rather than formulating responses while others spoke, he focused on fully understanding their perspectives before offering his input.

- Non-Judgmental Awareness: Alex cultivated non-judgmental awareness of his own communication patterns.

Instead of harsh self-criticism, he observed his habits with curiosity and openness.

Outcomes:

- Improved Relationships: Mindful communication contributed to improved relationships with colleagues. Alex's colleagues noted a positive shift in the quality of interactions, citing increased understanding and reduced misunderstandings.

- Enhanced Decision-Making: The practice of pausing and reflecting before responding enhanced Alex's decision-making abilities. He approached challenges with a clearer mindset, free from the automatic reactions that had previously clouded his judgment.

- Increased Emotional Intelligence: Mindful communication deepened Alex's emotional intelligence. He became more attuned to the emotions of himself and others, fostering a workplace environment characterized by empathy and collaboration.

Overcoming Challenges in Mindfulness Practice

While mindfulness holds transformative potential, individuals may encounter challenges in breaking free from autopilot habits. Addressing these challenges contributes to the sustainability and effectiveness of mindfulness practice:

Challenge: Impatience with Progress Strategy: Embrace the journey as a gradual process. Breaking autopilot habits through mindfulness is a journey of self-discovery, and progress may unfold at its own pace. Celebrate small victories and recognize that each moment of awareness contributes to positive change.

Challenge: Distractions and Multitasking Strategy: Create intentional spaces for mindfulness practice. Minimize distractions during dedicated mindfulness sessions and gradually extend mindful awareness to daily activities. Mindfulness is about being fully present, and minimizing multitasking enhances the depth of awareness.

Challenge: Resistance to Change Strategy: Approach mindfulness with an open mind. Resistance to change is a common barrier. Recognize that mindfulness is not about changing who you are but about becoming more aware of your habits and choices. Cultivate a mindset of curiosity and acceptance.

Challenge: Overthinking Mindfulness Strategy: Simplify mindfulness practices. Overthinking the practice can create unnecessary barriers. Start with simple exercises, such as mindful breathing or body scan meditations, and gradually explore more complex practices. The essence is to bring awareness to the present moment.

Conclusion: Liberating the Present from Automaticity

As we explore the landscape of autopilot habits and the transformative power of mindfulness, let the present moment become a canvas for liberation. Breaking free from automatic responses opens the door to intentional living, where each choice is infused with awareness and purpose.

May the practice of mindfulness be a compass, guiding us away from the inertia of unconscious habits and toward the freedom of conscious choice. As we transition to the subsequent chapters, let the essence of mindfulness linger—a reminder that in the vast canvas of each moment, the brush of awareness can paint a masterpiece of intentional and mindful living.

Getting Centered Through Meditation

In the chaotic dance of modern life, finding a sanctuary of stillness within becomes a transformative journey. Meditation, a timeless practice that spans cultures and traditions, serves as a gateway to inner peace, clarity, and mindfulness. In this exploration, we delve into the art and science of getting centered through meditation, unraveling the multifaceted benefits, diverse techniques, and the profound impact of this practice on our mental, emotional, and spiritual well-being.

The Essence of Meditation

At its core, meditation is a practice of cultivating awareness, presence, and a heightened state of consciousness. Rooted in ancient spiritual traditions, meditation has evolved and adapted to contemporary contexts, becoming a versatile tool for navigating the challenges of the modern world. The essence of meditation lies in the intentional focus of attention, whether on the breath, a mantra, or the present moment, fostering a state of deep presence and stillness.

The Science Behind Meditation

The transformative power of meditation extends beyond spiritual and philosophical realms to the realm of science. A growing body of research highlights the neurological, psychological, and physiological changes that occur during meditation:

Neuroplasticity: Meditation has been linked to changes in the brain's structure and function, a phenomenon known as neuroplasticity. Regular meditation is associated with increased gray matter density in brain regions related to memory, self-awareness, and compassion.

Cortical Thickness: Studies suggest that meditation may influence cortical thickness, particularly in areas associated with attention, sensory processing, and emotional regulation. These changes may contribute to enhanced cognitive functions and emotional well-being.

Stress Response: Meditation has a profound impact on the body's stress response. Mindful practices, such as mindfulness-based stress reduction (MBSR), have been shown to reduce cortisol levels, decrease perceived stress, and enhance overall resilience to stressors.

Emotional Regulation: The practice of meditation is linked to improvements in emotional regulation. Functional magnetic resonance imaging (fMRI) studies indicate changes in the amygdala, a brain region involved in processing emotions, suggesting that meditation may influence emotional reactivity.

Enhanced Attention and Concentration: Meditation has been associated with improvements in attention, concentration, and cognitive performance. Mindfulness practices, in particular, enhance the ability to sustain attention and resist distractions.

Types of Meditation Practices

Meditation is a diverse tapestry of practices, each offering a unique approach to cultivating mindfulness and centeredness. Let's explore some of the prominent meditation techniques that individuals can incorporate into their daily lives:

Mindfulness Meditation:

- Focus: Mindfulness meditation involves bringing attention to the present moment without judgment. Practitioners often focus on the breath, bodily sensations, or a specific point of awareness.

- Benefits: Enhances present-moment awareness, reduces stress, and fosters a non-judgmental mindset.

Loving-Kindness Meditation:

- Focus: Loving-kindness meditation, also known as "Metta," involves cultivating feelings of love and compassion toward oneself and others. Practitioners often repeat phrases or affirmations that express goodwill.

- Benefits: Cultivates compassion, fosters positive emotions, and contributes to a sense of interconnectedness.

Transcendental Meditation (TM):

- Focus: TM involves the silent repetition of a mantra, a specific word or sound, with the aim of transcending ordinary thought and entering a state of pure awareness.

- Benefits: Promotes relaxation, reduces stress, and is associated with improvements in overall well-being.

Body Scan Meditation:

- Focus: Body scan meditation involves systematically directing attention to different parts of the body, bringing awareness to physical sensations.

- Benefits: Enhances body awareness, promotes relaxation, and can be effective in managing chronic pain or tension.

Guided Meditation:

- Focus: In guided meditation, a narrator or guide leads participants through visualizations, affirmations, or mindfulness exercises.

- Benefits: Suitable for beginners, fosters relaxation, and can address specific goals such as stress reduction or personal development.

Zen Meditation (Zazen):

- Focus: Zazen, a central practice in Zen Buddhism, involves seated meditation with a focus on breath awareness or koans (paradoxical statements or questions).

- Benefits: Cultivates concentration, clarity, and insight. Emphasizes the experience of "just sitting."

The Practice: Getting Started with Meditation

Embarking on a meditation practice is a personal and evolving journey. Whether you are a seasoned practitioner or new to meditation, here are practical steps to get started and deepen your experience:

Create a Sacred Space:

- Designate a quiet and comfortable space for your meditation practice. This can be a corner of a room, a cushion, or a chair. Personalize the space with items that evoke a sense of peace and tranquility.

Choose a Comfortable Posture:

- Find a posture that allows you to be both alert and relaxed. This can be a seated position on the floor or a chair, or even lying down if that is more comfortable. Keep the spine straight and the body relaxed.

Set an Intention:

- Begin each meditation session by setting a clear intention. This could be a specific focus, such as cultivating gratitude or finding inner peace. Setting an intention provides a sense of purpose to your practice.

Start with Breath Awareness:

- For beginners, start with breath awareness. Focus on the natural rhythm of your breath, observing the inhalation and exhalation. When the mind wanders, gently bring it back to the breath.

Experiment with Different Techniques:
- Explore various meditation techniques to find what resonates with you. Whether it's mindfulness, loving-kindness, or transcendental meditation, the key is to find a practice that aligns with your preferences and goals.

Be Consistent:
- Consistency is key to reaping the benefits of meditation. Start with short sessions and gradually extend the duration as you become more comfortable. Aim for a daily practice to build a sustainable habit.

Mindful Movement as Meditation:
- Meditation is not limited to sitting practices. Engage in mindful movement, such as walking meditation or yoga, as a form of meditation. The key is to bring full awareness to the movement and sensations.

The Transformative Benefits of Meditation

The practice of getting centered through meditation extends beyond the immediate moments of stillness, influencing various dimensions of well-being:

Stress Reduction:
- Meditation is renowned for its stress-reducing effects. By inducing a state of relaxation and promoting a calm mind, meditation helps mitigate the physiological and psychological impacts of stress.

Enhanced Emotional Well-Being:

- Regular meditation is associated with improved emotional regulation. Practitioners often report heightened levels of positive emotions, increased resilience, and a greater capacity to navigate challenging emotions.

Improved Focus and Concentration:

- The focused attention cultivated in meditation contributes to improved concentration and cognitive performance. Individuals who practice meditation often exhibit enhanced attentional control and reduced mind-wandering.

Enhanced Self-Awareness:

- Meditation is a journey inward, fostering a deepened sense of self-awareness. Practitioners become attuned to their thoughts, emotions, and habitual patterns, enabling greater self-understanding and personal growth.

Cultivation of Compassion:

- Loving-kindness meditation, in particular, emphasizes the cultivation of compassion toward oneself and others. This practice contributes to a more empathetic and connected way of relating to oneself and the world.

Mind-Body Connection:

- Meditation promotes a profound connection between the mind and body. As individuals become more attuned to bodily sensations and the present moment, they often experience a sense of groundedness and holistic well-being.

Practical Tips for Overcoming Challenges in Meditation

While the benefits of meditation are vast, individuals may encounter challenges along the way. Addressing these challenges enhances the sustainability and effectiveness of the practice:

Challenge: Restlessness or Impatience Strategy: Embrace restlessness as part of the process. Instead of resisting, observe restlessness with curiosity. Experiment with dynamic meditation techniques, such as mindful movement or walking meditation, to channel excess energy.

Challenge: Wandering Mind Strategy: Gently redirect the mind. When the mind wanders, avoid self-judgment. Gently guide your attention back to the chosen point of focus, whether it's the breath, a mantra, or a visual anchor.

Challenge: Lack of Time Strategy: Prioritize consistency over duration. Even brief meditation sessions can be impactful. Incorporate meditation into daily routines, such as during breaks, in the morning, or before bedtime.

Challenge: Physical Discomfort Strategy: Find a comfortable posture. Experiment with different cushions, chairs, or meditation benches to alleviate physical discomfort. Gentle stretches or yoga before meditation can also enhance comfort.

Challenge: Overemphasis on "Success" Strategy: Redefine success in meditation. Rather than focusing on achieving a particular state, consider success as the commitment to showing up for your practice. Let go of expectations and allow the practice to unfold.

Conclusion: The Journey Within

As we navigate the landscape of getting centered through meditation, let the journey within be a sanctuary for self-discovery, tranquility, and mindful presence. In the stillness of meditation, we find a refuge from the demands of the external world and an opportunity to reconnect with the essence of our being.

May the practice of meditation be a compass, guiding us back to the present moment and unveiling the profound interconnectedness of all things. As we transition to the subsequent chapters, let the essence of meditation linger—a reminder that within the sanctuary of our own awareness, we have the power to cultivate a life of presence, purpose, and profound centeredness.

Body Scans for Calm Presence

In the hustle and bustle of daily life, the body often becomes a silent witness to the stresses and strains we encounter. Mindfulness, with its emphasis on present-moment awareness, offers a powerful tool to reconnect with the body and foster a sense of calm presence. Body scan meditation, a specific mindfulness practice, invites individuals to explore and cultivate awareness of sensations throughout the body. In this exploration, we delve into the nuances of body scans, their benefits, and how they serve as a pathway to a grounded and tranquil state of being.

The Art of Body Scan Meditation

Body scan meditation is a form of mindfulness practice that involves systematically directing attention to different parts of the body, from head to toe. The aim is to bring awareness to the sensations present in each region without judgment, allowing for a deepening connection between the mind and body. This practice is rooted in the principle that the body holds valuable information and wisdom, and by turning attention inward, individuals can cultivate a heightened sense of presence and relaxation.

The Mind-Body Connection

The mind-body connection is a fundamental aspect of body scan meditation. As thoughts, emotions, and sensations are intricately interwoven, bringing attention to the body becomes a gateway to understanding and influencing one's mental and emotional states. The mind-body connection is supported by scientific evidence, illustrating the profound impact of mental states on bodily functions and vice versa.

Psychophysiological Effects:

- Stress Reduction: Body scan meditation is associated with reduced physiological markers of stress, including decreased cortisol levels and heart rate. By fostering relaxation, this practice contributes to a calmer nervous system.

- Pain Management: In the realm of chronic pain, body scan meditation has been shown to be effective in reducing pain intensity and improving pain-related outcomes. By directing attention away from pain and toward bodily sensations, individuals may experience relief.

- Immune System Support: Mindfulness practices, including body scan meditation, have been linked to improvements in immune system function. The mind's influence on immune response underscores the holistic nature of the mind-body connection.

The Anatomy of Body Scan Meditation

The practice of body scan meditation unfolds in a deliberate and systematic manner. While variations exist, the following framework provides a general guide to the anatomy of a body scan:

Preparation:

- Set the Intention: Begin the practice by setting a clear intention. This could involve cultivating awareness, promoting relaxation, or simply being present with the body.

- Comfortable Posture: Find a comfortable position, whether sitting or lying down. The goal is to be at ease while maintaining a sense of alertness.

Beginning the Scan:

- Focus on the Breath: Start by bringing attention to the breath. This initial focus serves as an anchor, grounding the mind in the present moment.

- Head to Toe Exploration: Begin scanning the body from the top of the head down to the toes. Move slowly and deliberately, paying attention to each region.

Guidance and Awareness:

- Guided Instructions: Some individuals find it helpful to use guided instructions, either through recordings or a meditation guide. These instructions may prompt attention to specific areas and encourage a gentle, non-judgmental awareness.

- Sensory Exploration: As attention moves through each part of the body, individuals are encouraged to notice sensations without attachment or aversion. Sensations may include warmth, tingling, tension, or areas of discomfort.

Deepening Awareness:

- Breath and Release: In areas of tension or discomfort, individuals can use the breath as a tool for release. Inhale a sense of spaciousness, and on the exhale, allow tension to dissipate.

- Body as Landscape: Visualize the body as a landscape, exploring the hills and valleys of sensations. This metaphorical approach enhances the experiential nature of the practice.

Closing the Scan:

- Full Body Awareness: Conclude the body scan by expanding awareness to the entire body. Feel the body as a unified whole, present and anchored in the current moment.

- Gratitude and Reflection: Express gratitude for the body and the opportunity to cultivate awareness. Reflect on any insights or shifts in sensations that arose during the practice.

Benefits of Body Scan Meditation

Body scan meditation offers a myriad of benefits that extend beyond the immediate practice. Incorporating this mindfulness technique into a regular routine can contribute to overall well-being:

Stress Reduction and Relaxation:

- Tension Release: By systematically scanning and releasing tension in different parts of the body, individuals experience a profound sense of relaxation. This, in turn, contributes to stress reduction and a calmer nervous system.

- Cortisol Regulation: Body scan meditation has been linked to decreased cortisol levels, a hormone associated with stress. This hormonal regulation supports a more balanced and resilient stress response.

- Improved Sleep: Practicing body scans, particularly before bedtime, can promote relaxation and contribute to improved sleep quality. The release of bodily tension creates an environment conducive to restful sleep.

Enhanced Mindfulness and Presence:

- Cultivation of Mindfulness: Body scan meditation is a powerful tool for cultivating mindfulness—the ability to be fully present in the current moment. As attention is directed to bodily sensations, the mind becomes anchored in the here and now.

- Interrupting Thought Patterns: The practice of body scan serves as a gentle interruption to habitual thought patterns. By shifting attention from the thinking mind to bodily sensations, individuals experience a temporary respite from mental chatter.

Emotional Regulation:

- Body-Sensation Awareness: The practice of attending to bodily sensations fosters a heightened awareness of emotions stored in the body. This awareness contributes to emotional regulation by allowing individuals to observe and respond to emotions in a conscious and intentional manner.

- Grounding in the Present: The anchoring effect of body scan meditation provides a grounding experience. This grounded presence can be particularly beneficial during moments of heightened emotional intensity.

Mind-Body Harmony:

- Holistic Well-Being: Body scan meditation nurtures a sense of holistic well-being by acknowledging the interconnectedness of mind and body. As individuals develop a deeper understanding of the mind-body connection, they are better equipped to navigate various dimensions of health.

- Somatic Wisdom: The body holds a reservoir of somatic wisdom—insights and intuitions that go beyond intellectual understanding. Body scan meditation allows individuals to tap into this wisdom, fostering a harmonious relationship between body and mind.

Practical Tips for Body Scan Meditation

Embarking on a journey of body scan meditation requires a willingness to explore and a commitment to regular practice. Here are practical tips to enhance the effectiveness of body scan meditation:

Start Gradually:

- For beginners, start with shorter body scan sessions and gradually extend the duration as comfort and familiarity with the practice grow.

Mindful Breath Integration:

- Integrate mindful breathing into the body scan. Use the breath as an anchor, synchronizing each breath with the exploration of different body regions.

Non-Judgmental Observation:

- Approach sensations with a non-judgmental and curious awareness. Avoid labeling sensations as "good" or "bad." Instead, observe them as they are, allowing a spacious and open-minded awareness.

Regular Consistency:

- Aim for regular consistency in practice. Set aside dedicated time for body scan meditation, and experiment with different times of the day to find what suits your routine.

Experiment with Guided Sessions:

- Explore guided body scan meditations led by experienced instructors. Guided sessions provide structure and support, especially for those new to the practice.

Adapt to Preferences:

- Customize the practice to suit personal preferences. Some individuals may prefer to focus on specific areas of the body, while others may enjoy a more comprehensive head-to-toe exploration.

Combination with Other Practices:

- Combine body scan meditation with other mindfulness practices. For example, follow a body scan with mindful movement or loving-kindness meditation to create a holistic approach to well-being.

Case Studies: Navigating Stress Through Body Scan Meditation

Case Study 1: Emma's Stress Reduction Journey

Background: Emma, a software engineer, experienced chronic stress due to demanding work deadlines and a busy lifestyle.

Body Scan Meditation Practice:

- Daily Routine: Emma incorporated a ten-minute body scan meditation into her daily routine. She practiced in the evening to unwind from the day's stressors.

- Focus on Tension Release: During the body scan, Emma intentionally focused on areas of tension, especially in her shoulders and neck. With each breath, she visualized releasing tightness and inviting a sense of ease.

Outcomes:

- Improved Sleep Quality: Emma noticed a significant improvement in her sleep quality. The practice of body scan meditation helped her transition from a state of heightened alertness to a more relaxed and restful state before bedtime.

- Enhanced Stress Resilience: Regular body scan sessions contributed to Emma's resilience to workplace stress. She found herself approaching challenges with a greater sense of calm and clarity.

Case Study 2: Mark's Pain Management Journey

Background: Mark, a teacher, struggled with chronic lower back pain, exacerbated by long hours of standing in the classroom.

Body Scan Meditation Practice:

- Targeted Attention: Mark tailored his body scan practice to focus specifically on his lower back. During the meditation, he directed mindful attention to sensations in this area, observing without judgment.

- Breath as a Soothing Tool: In moments of discomfort, Mark used his breath as a soothing tool. Deep inhalations were accompanied by a mental release of tension, creating a sense of spaciousness in the lower back.

Outcomes:

- Pain Reduction: Mark experienced a noticeable reduction in lower back pain. The combination of body scan meditation and intentional breathwork contributed to increased awareness of his body and a more relaxed state.

- Improved Posture: The heightened awareness cultivated through body scan meditation translated into improved posture during daily activities. Mark found himself adopting a more ergonomic stance, minimizing strain on his lower back.

Overcoming Challenges in Body Scan Meditation

While body scan meditation offers profound benefits, individuals may encounter challenges along the way. Addressing these challenges enhances the sustainability and effectiveness of the practice:

Challenge: Restlessness or Impatience Strategy: Embrace restlessness as part of the process. Instead of resisting, observe restlessness with curiosity. Allow the body scan to unfold at its own pace, and avoid rushing through the practice.

Challenge: Distractions Strategy: Gently redirect attention. If the mind becomes distracted during the body scan, gently guide attention back to the chosen area. Use the breath as an anchor to ground awareness.

Challenge: Discomfort or Pain Strategy: Approach discomfort with compassion. If sensations of discomfort or pain arise, approach them with a gentle and compassionate awareness. Use the breath to soothe and create a sense of spaciousness.

Challenge: Inconsistent Practice Strategy: Prioritize consistency over duration. Even short body scan sessions can be beneficial. Experiment with different times of the day to find when the practice integrates most seamlessly into your routine.

Challenge: Mental Chatter Strategy: Acknowledge and release mental chatter. If the mind is actively generating thoughts during the body scan, acknowledge them without judgment and gently guide attention back to bodily sensations.

Conclusion: A Journey of Embodied Presence

As we explore the realm of body scan meditation, may it be a guide on the journey to embodied presence—a state where the mind and body harmonize in the dance of awareness. In the tapestry of sensations, may each breath be a brushstroke, painting a masterpiece of tranquility and self-discovery.

May the practice of body scan meditation be a sanctuary, inviting us to explore the rich terrain of our own embodied experience. As we transition to the subsequent chapters, let the essence of body scan meditation linger—a reminder that in the gentle attention to our own bodies, we discover a gateway to calm presence and a profound connection to the present moment.

Loving-Kindness Toward Self and Others

In the tapestry of mindfulness practices, loving-kindness meditation stands out as a radiant thread—a practice that illuminates the path to compassion, connection, and profound well-being. Rooted in ancient contemplative traditions, loving-kindness meditation, also known as "Metta," invites individuals to cultivate a boundless and unconditional love toward oneself and others. In this exploration, we delve into the essence of loving-kindness, its transformative effects, and how it serves as a bridge to fostering compassion in our relationships with both ourselves and the world.

The Heart of Loving-Kindness Meditation

At its core, loving-kindness meditation is a practice of generating and radiating love, goodwill, and benevolence. The origins of this practice can be traced back to various contemplative traditions, including Buddhism and Hinduism, where it is recognized as a transformative tool for cultivating a compassionate heart. The essence of loving-kindness lies in its inclusive nature—it extends beyond personal relationships to encompass all beings, fostering a sense of interconnectedness.

The Practice: Cultivating Loving-Kindness

Loving-kindness meditation typically follows a structured sequence of phrases and intentions, with the aim of progressively expanding the circle of compassion. While variations exist, the foundational elements of the practice include:

Self-Compassion:

- Begin by directing loving-kindness toward oneself. This involves offering heartfelt wishes for one's well-being, happiness, and freedom from suffering. Phrases such as "May I be happy, may I be healthy, may I be safe, may I be at ease" are commonly used.

Expanding to Others:
- The practice then extends to loved ones, acquaintances, neutral individuals, and even those with whom there may be challenges. The phrases are adapted accordingly, such as "May you be happy, may you be healthy," and so forth.

Culmination in Universal Compassion:
- The culmination of loving-kindness meditation involves extending benevolent wishes to all beings without exception. The phrases become expansive, embracing the entirety of humanity and beyond: "May all beings be happy, may all beings be healthy."

Visualization and Sensation:
- Practitioners often incorporate visualization to enhance the sense of connection. This may involve imagining a warm, radiant light emanating from the heart, enveloping oneself and extending to others. Sensations of love and warmth are cultivated and nurtured.

Scientific Insights: The Impact of Loving-Kindness

Beyond its spiritual roots, loving-kindness meditation has captured the attention of scientists exploring the intersection of mindfulness and well-being. Research studies have highlighted the following insights into the impact of loving-kindness meditation:

Positive Emotion Enhancement:

- Loving-kindness meditation is associated with increased positive emotions, including love, joy, gratitude, and compassion. Regular practice contributes to a more positive emotional outlook and greater emotional resilience.

Reduction in Negative Emotions:
- The practice has been linked to a reduction in negative emotions such as anger, resentment, and stress. By cultivating love and goodwill, individuals may experience a shift away from habitual negative emotional patterns.

Improved Emotional Regulation:
- Loving-kindness meditation enhances emotional regulation by fostering a compassionate response to one's own emotions and the emotions of others. This can contribute to greater emotional intelligence and empathy.

Enhanced Well-Being:
- Studies suggest that the regular practice of loving-kindness meditation is associated with improvements in overall well-being and life satisfaction. Cultivating a positive and compassionate mindset contributes to a more fulfilling and meaningful life.

Changes in Brain Structure:
- Neuroscientific research indicates that loving-kindness meditation may lead to changes in brain structure, particularly in areas associated with emotional processing and empathy. These changes support the cultivation of a compassionate mindset.

Loving-Kindness Toward Oneself: The Foundation

The journey of loving-kindness begins with the practice of extending benevolence toward oneself. In a world often marked by self-criticism and unrealistic expectations, cultivating self-compassion becomes a cornerstone of well-being. Let's explore the transformative power of loving-kindness toward oneself:

Embracing Imperfections:

- Loving-kindness toward oneself involves embracing imperfections and acknowledging one's humanity. The practice encourages a gentle and non-judgmental attitude toward one's shortcomings and challenges.

Self-Kindness in Adversity:

- During difficult times, loving-kindness meditation becomes a refuge of self-kindness. Instead of succumbing to self-blame or harsh judgment, individuals offer themselves the same compassion they would extend to a dear friend facing similar challenges.

Cultivating a Positive Self-Image:

- Regular practice contributes to the cultivation of a positive self-image. The phrases used in loving-kindness meditation serve as affirmations that reinforce feelings of self-worth, deserving happiness, and being deserving of love.

Healing Inner Wounds:

- For those carrying emotional scars or wounds from the past, loving-kindness becomes a healing balm. By directing compassion toward areas of pain, individuals initiate a process of inner healing and self-acceptance.

Mindful Self-Care Practices:

- Loving-kindness toward oneself extends beyond the meditation cushion to mindful self-care practices. This involves making choices that prioritize well-being, setting boundaries, and engaging in activities that nourish the body, mind, and soul.

Extending Compassion to Others: A Ripple Effect

As the practice of loving-kindness takes root within, its natural progression is to extend compassion outward, creating a ripple effect that touches the lives of others. Let's explore how loving-kindness toward others becomes a transformative force in relationships and communities:

Enhanced Empathy:

- Loving-kindness meditation cultivates empathy by encouraging individuals to consider the experiences and emotions of others. This enhanced empathy lays the foundation for more compassionate and understanding relationships.

Resolving Interpersonal Conflict:

- In moments of conflict or tension, the practice of loving-kindness becomes a valuable tool. Individuals can intentionally extend compassionate wishes to those with whom they may have differences, fostering a mindset of reconciliation and understanding.

Building Positive Connections:

- The practice contributes to the building of positive and supportive connections with others. As individuals radiate love and goodwill, they often find that these qualities are reciprocated, creating a positive and harmonious social environment.

Cultivating Patience and Tolerance:

- Loving-kindness meditation nurtures qualities of patience and tolerance. When faced with the challenges of interpersonal relationships, individuals may draw upon the reservoir of compassion cultivated through the practice, fostering resilience and understanding.

Contributing to Collective Well-Being:

- The ripple effect of loving-kindness extends beyond individual relationships to contribute to collective well-being. As more individuals embrace a compassionate mindset, communities and societies may experience a positive shift toward harmony and cooperation.

Practical Tips for Loving-Kindness Meditation

Embarking on the journey of loving-kindness meditation involves a commitment to regular practice and an open-hearted willingness to cultivate compassion. Here are practical tips to enhance the effectiveness of loving-kindness meditation:

Begin with Self-Compassion:

- Start the practice by directing loving-kindness toward yourself. This foundation of self-compassion sets the tone for extending benevolence to others.

Adapt Phrases to Suit Your Feelings:

- Modify the phrases used in loving-kindness meditation to resonate with your authentic feelings. Choose words that genuinely evoke a sense of love and goodwill.

Start with Small Circles:

- If the practice feels challenging, begin with smaller circles of individuals. Start with loved ones, then gradually extend to acquaintances, neutral individuals, and, ultimately, all beings.

Incorporate Visualization:

- Enhance the practice by incorporating visualization. Imagine a warm, radiant light emanating from your heart, enveloping yourself and others in a cocoon of love and compassion.

Experiment with Different Postures:
- Explore different postures for loving-kindness meditation. While traditionally practiced in a seated position, you may find that lying down or even walking enhances your experience of the practice.

Integrate Loving-Kindness into Daily Life:
- Extend the practice of loving-kindness beyond formal meditation sessions. Infuse moments of daily life with benevolent wishes, whether it's during a challenging meeting, a commute, or a quiet moment of reflection.

Combine with Mindful Breathing:
- Integrate mindful breathing into loving-kindness meditation. Use the breath as an anchor, allowing each breath to carry and amplify feelings of love and goodwill.

Case Studies: The Transformative Power of Loving-Kindness

Case Study 1: Sarah's Journey to Self-Compassion

Background: Sarah, a marketing professional, struggled with perfectionism and self-criticism, impacting her overall well-being.

Loving-Kindness Meditation Practice:
- Focus on Self-Compassion: Sarah began her loving-kindness meditation practice by placing a strong emphasis on cultivating self-compassion. She used phrases like "May I be gentle with myself," and "May I embrace imperfections."

Outcomes:
- Shift in Self-Perception: Over time, Sarah experienced a significant shift in her self-perception. The practice of loving-kindness became a powerful antidote to

self-critical thoughts, fostering self-acceptance and a more positive self-image.

- Increased Resilience: As Sarah faced challenges at work, the practice of loving-kindness provided a resilient mindset. Instead of being overwhelmed by perfectionist tendencies, she approached tasks with a greater sense of ease and self-compassion.

Case Study 2: James' Journey to Reconciliation

Background: James, a teacher, experienced tension and conflict with a colleague, impacting the work environment.

Loving-Kindness Meditation Practice:

- Directed Compassion Toward Colleague: James adapted his loving-kindness meditation to include his colleague. During the practice, he intentionally directed benevolent wishes toward the colleague, using phrases like "May you find peace" and "May our relationship be harmonious."

Outcomes:

- Shift in Perspective: The practice of loving-kindness facilitated a shift in James' perspective. Instead of viewing the colleague through a lens of conflict, he began to see common humanity and shared aspirations, fostering understanding.

- Improved Communication: James found that as he continued the loving-kindness meditation, communication with the colleague improved. The practice contributed to a more empathetic and patient approach, creating space for resolution and collaboration.

Overcoming Challenges in Loving-Kindness Meditation

While the practice of loving-kindness meditation holds transformative potential, individuals may encounter challenges along the way. Addressing these challenges enhances the sustainability and effectiveness of the practice:

Challenge: Emotional Discomfort Strategy: Approach emotional discomfort with gentleness. If challenging emotions arise during the practice, meet them with a compassionate awareness. Use the phrases to cultivate a sense of safety and ease.

Challenge: Limited Feelings of Love Strategy: Start where you are. If feelings of love or goodwill are limited, begin by acknowledging and accepting your current emotional state. The practice is a journey, and genuine feelings of love may develop over time.

Challenge: Impatience or Frustration Strategy: Embrace the practice as a process. If impatience or frustration arises, acknowledge these emotions without judgment. The journey of loving-kindness is gradual, and each moment of intentional compassion contributes to the overall transformation.

Challenge: Skepticism or Resistance Strategy: Explore the resistance with curiosity. If skepticism or resistance emerges, inquire into the underlying beliefs or narratives. Consider reframing the practice as an experiment and be open to the possibility of positive change.

Challenge: Time Constraints Strategy: Prioritize consistency over duration. Even brief sessions of loving-kindness meditation can be beneficial. Integrate the practice into daily routines, finding moments for benevolent wishes during everyday activities.

Conclusion: Radiating Compassion in Every Breath

As we navigate the landscape of loving-kindness meditation, may each breath become a vessel of compassion—a reminder that within the simple act of extending benevolence, we uncover a boundless reservoir of love. In the symphony of connection, may the practice of loving-kindness be a melody that harmonizes the heart with the world.

May the essence of loving-kindness linger as we transition to the subsequent chapters—a beacon of compassion illuminating the path toward greater self-discovery, interconnectedness, and a world where the transformative power of love extends to every corner of our lives.

Chapter 4: Fueling Positivity Through Movement
Neuroscience of Exercise

In the dance between the mind and body, the rhythm of movement plays a vital role in orchestrating a symphony of well-being. The marriage of neuroscience and exercise illuminates the intricate ways in which physical activity shapes not only our bodies but also our brains. As we explore the neuroscience of exercise, we delve into the profound impact of movement on brain health, cognitive function, and emotional well-being. This exploration serves as a gateway to understanding how regular exercise becomes a potent elixir, fueling positivity and enhancing the overall quality of life.

The Brain-Body Connection

The brain and body are intimately connected, engaged in a constant dialogue that influences various aspects of our health and functioning. The bidirectional relationship between the brain and the body is particularly pronounced when it comes to exercise. Let's unravel the interconnected web of the brain-body connection:

Neurotransmitters and Mood Regulation:
- Exercise acts as a powerful modulator of neurotransmitters—chemical messengers in the brain that play a crucial role in mood regulation. During physical activity, the brain releases neurotransmitters such as serotonin, dopamine, and norepinephrine, which contribute to feelings of happiness, pleasure, and reduced stress.

Endorphins: The Feel-Good Hormones:
- Endorphins, often referred to as the body's natural painkillers, are released during exercise. These neurochemicals produce a euphoric sensation, commonly

known as the "runner's high," contributing to an overall sense of well-being and contentment.

Brain-Derived Neurotrophic Factor (BDNF):

- Exercise stimulates the production of Brain-Derived Neurotrophic Factor (BDNF), a protein that supports the growth, survival, and function of neurons (nerve cells). Increased levels of BDNF are associated with improved cognitive function, enhanced mood, and a reduced risk of neurodegenerative disorders.

Cortisol Regulation:

- Cortisol, a hormone released in response to stress, is regulated through exercise. Regular physical activity helps maintain healthy cortisol levels, preventing the detrimental effects of chronic stress on the brain, such as impaired memory and increased anxiety.

Hippocampal Neurogenesis:

- The hippocampus, a region of the brain critical for learning and memory, undergoes neurogenesis— the formation of new neurons— in response to exercise. This process is linked to cognitive resilience, improved memory, and a reduced risk of age-related cognitive decline.

Impact of Exercise on Cognitive Function

The cognitive benefits of exercise extend beyond mood regulation to encompass various aspects of mental functioning. Whether it's sharpening focus, boosting creativity, or enhancing problem-solving skills, the impact of movement on cognitive function is a testament to the holistic nature of the brain-body connection:

Executive Function and Decision-Making:

- Regular exercise is associated with improved executive functions, which include cognitive processes such as decision-making, planning, and problem-solving. The enhanced blood flow and neurochemical changes induced by exercise contribute to optimal cognitive performance.

Attention and Concentration:

- Physical activity has been shown to positively influence attention and concentration. Whether it's a brisk walk, a workout session, or a yoga practice, the engagement of the body in movement enhances the brain's ability to focus and sustain attention.

Memory Enhancement:

- Exercise is a catalyst for memory enhancement. The hippocampus, a key player in the formation and retrieval of memories, benefits from increased blood flow and neurogenesis induced by physical activity. As a result, individuals who engage in regular exercise often experience improvements in both short-term and long-term memory.

Cognitive Flexibility:

- Cognitive flexibility, the ability to adapt and switch between different tasks and mental processes, is influenced by exercise. The neuroplasticity facilitated by physical activity supports the brain's capacity to adapt to new information and challenges, fostering cognitive flexibility.

Creativity and Brain Connectivity:

- Movement has been linked to increased creativity, with research suggesting that engaging in physical activity enhances divergent thinking—the ability to generate a variety of ideas. Exercise also promotes connectivity between different regions of the brain, fostering a creative and integrated thought process.

Exercise as a Stress Resilience Tool

In the fast-paced and often stressful landscape of modern life, exercise emerges as a potent tool for stress resilience. The neurobiological mechanisms through which exercise mitigates the impact of stress contribute to both mental and physical well-being:

Stress-Buffering Effect:

- Exercise serves as a natural stress-buffering agent. Physical activity triggers the release of endorphins, which counteract the physiological and psychological effects of stress. The feel-good sensations induced by endorphins create a protective shield against the negative impact of stressors.

Hormonal Regulation:

- Cortisol, the primary stress hormone, is regulated through exercise. While acute stress prompts a temporary increase in cortisol levels, regular physical activity helps maintain a healthy balance. This hormonal regulation contributes to a more adaptive stress response.

Reduction of Anxiety and Depression:

- Exercise has been consistently linked to a reduction in symptoms of anxiety and depression. The neurochemical changes induced by physical activity, along with the positive impact on neurotransmitters, create an environment conducive to emotional well-being.

Mind-Body Relaxation Response:

- Engaging in activities such as yoga or mindful movement activates the parasympathetic nervous system, triggering a relaxation response. This counteracts the fight-or-flight response associated with stress, promoting a state of calm and equilibrium.

Sleep Quality Improvement:

- Sleep, a critical component of stress resilience, is positively influenced by exercise. The physical and mental exertion during exercise contributes to improved sleep quality, further enhancing the body's ability to recover from stress.

Tailoring Exercise for Positivity: From Cardio to Mindful Movement

The diversity of exercise modalities offers individuals the flexibility to choose activities that align with their preferences and goals. Whether it's the invigorating rhythm of cardiovascular exercise or the mindful flow of practices like yoga, each modality brings its unique set of benefits to the neuroscientific table:

Cardiovascular Exercise:

- Aerobic or cardiovascular exercise, such as running, cycling, or brisk walking, is associated with the release of endorphins and improved mood. The sustained nature of cardiovascular exercise enhances blood flow to the brain, promoting cognitive function and overall mental well-being.

Strength Training and Neuroplasticity:

- Strength training, which involves resistance exercises like weightlifting, contributes to neuroplasticity—the brain's ability to reorganize and adapt. This form of exercise is linked to improved cognitive function, especially in tasks requiring working memory and executive function.

Mindful Movement Practices:

- Mindful movement practices, including yoga and tai chi, integrate physical activity with a contemplative approach. These practices not only enhance flexibility and strength but also cultivate mindfulness—the awareness of the present moment. The combination of movement and mindfulness contributes to stress reduction and emotional balance.

Dance Therapy:

- Dance, as a form of expressive movement, holds therapeutic value for mental and emotional well-being. The combination of music, rhythm, and physical expression engages multiple brain regions, fostering creativity, emotional release, and a sense of joy.

Outdoor Activities and Nature Connection:

- Engaging in exercise outdoors, whether it's hiking, jogging, or simply walking, amplifies the positive effects of physical activity. Exposure to nature has been associated with reduced stress, improved mood, and increased feelings of vitality.

Personalizing the Exercise Prescription

Just as each individual is unique, so too is the response to exercise. Personalizing the exercise prescription involves considering factors such as individual preferences, fitness levels, health conditions, and lifestyle constraints. Here are key considerations for tailoring the exercise prescription:

Individual Preferences:

- Choose activities that resonate with personal interests and preferences. Whether it's the camaraderie of group fitness classes, the solitude of a solo run, or the meditative quality of yoga, enjoyment enhances adherence to regular exercise.

Gradual Progression:
- Gradually progress the intensity and duration of exercise. A gradual approach allows the body and mind to adapt, reducing the risk of injury and creating a sustainable exercise habit.

Balancing Modalities:
- Incorporate a mix of cardiovascular, strength training, and mindful movement practices. A balanced approach ensures comprehensive physical and mental benefits, addressing different aspects of well-being.

Adaptation to Health Conditions:
- Consider individual health conditions and adapt exercise accordingly. Individuals with specific health concerns or chronic conditions may benefit from consulting with healthcare professionals or fitness experts to tailor a safe and effective exercise plan.

Consistency Over Intensity:
- Prioritize consistency over intensity. Regular, moderate-intensity exercise is often more sustainable and beneficial in the long run than sporadic, high-intensity workouts. Consistency contributes to the cumulative positive effects of exercise on the brain and body.

Integration into Daily Routine:
- Integrate exercise into daily routines. Finding opportunities for movement throughout the day, such as taking short walks, using stairs, or incorporating stretching breaks, contributes to overall physical activity levels.

Case Studies: From Sedentary to Active Living

Case Study 1: Emily's Journey to Mood Enhancement

Background: Emily, a desk-bound professional, experienced persistent low mood and stress due to a sedentary lifestyle.

Exercise Intervention:

- Incorporating Daily Walks: Emily started by incorporating daily walks into her routine. During breaks at work, she took short walks around the office building, gradually increasing the duration.

Outcomes:

- Improved Mood: Within a few weeks, Emily noticed a significant improvement in her mood. The combination of fresh air, movement, and the release of endorphins during walks contributed to a more positive outlook.

Case Study 2: David's Cognitive Boost Through Strength Training

Background: David, a retiree, was concerned about cognitive decline and memory lapses.

Exercise Intervention:

- Regular Strength Training: David incorporated regular strength training sessions into his weekly routine. He focused on exercises targeting major muscle groups, gradually increasing resistance.

Outcomes:

- Enhanced Cognitive Function: Over several months, David experienced enhanced cognitive function. His memory and ability to focus improved, and he reported feeling mentally sharper and more alert.

Overcoming Barriers to Exercise Adherence

While the benefits of exercise are well-established, individuals may face barriers that impede adherence to a regular exercise routine. Identifying and addressing these barriers is crucial for creating sustainable habits:

Barrier: Lack of Time Strategy: Prioritize short, effective workouts. High-intensity interval training (HIIT) and efficient, full-body exercises can provide substantial benefits in shorter time frames.

Barrier: Lack of Motivation Strategy: Find activities that bring joy. Incorporating enjoyable and social elements into exercise, such as joining group classes or exercising with a friend, can boost motivation.

Barrier: Physical Limitations or Health Concerns Strategy: Consult healthcare professionals or fitness experts. Individuals with physical limitations or health concerns can benefit from personalized guidance to adapt exercises to their specific needs.

Barrier: Monotony and Boredom Strategy: Vary the exercise routine. Introducing variety, whether it's trying different forms of exercise or exploring outdoor activities, prevents boredom and keeps the experience engaging.

Barrier: Weather Constraints Strategy: Embrace indoor alternatives. Having a contingency plan for unfavorable weather, such as indoor workouts or activities, ensures that external factors don't derail the exercise routine.

Barrier: Lack of Social Support Strategy: Seek accountability and support. Joining fitness classes, exercising with a friend, or participating in community events creates a supportive environment that enhances adherence.

Conclusion: A Movement Manifesto for Positivity

As we conclude our exploration of the neuroscience of exercise, let the wisdom of movement resonate as a manifesto for positivity—a call to dance with the rhythms of well-being. In the fusion of mind and body, may the act of movement be a celebration of vitality, resilience, and the profound interconnectedness of our physical and mental realms.

May the journey into the world of exercise become an exploration—a vibrant tapestry of cardiovascular rhythms, strength symphonies, and mindful movements. As we transition to the subsequent chapters, let the spirit of movement linger—a reminder that in every step, we cultivate not only physical health but also the boundless positivity that arises from the alchemy of neuroscientific harmony.

Yoga Poses for Peace

In the ancient art of yoga, the union of mind, body, and breath unfolds in a symphony of postures, known as asanas. These poses, cultivated over millennia, offer not only physical benefits but also serve as gateways to inner peace and tranquility. In this exploration, we dive into the realm of yoga, unveiling a collection of poses specifically designed to evoke a sense of peace and harmony. As we embark on this journey, let the mat become a sacred space—a canvas for the artistry of movement and a sanctuary for cultivating serenity amidst the ebb and flow of life.

The Essence of Yoga: Beyond Physical Postures

Yoga, an ancient practice with roots in Indian philosophy, extends far beyond the physical postures commonly associated with it. At its core, yoga is a holistic system encompassing physical, mental, and spiritual dimensions. The physical aspect of yoga, represented by asanas, is just one limb of the eightfold path outlined in the Yoga Sutras of Patanjali.

In the pursuit of peace through yoga, it is essential to embrace the broader principles that guide the practice:

Breath Awareness (Pranayama):

- Pranayama, the practice of conscious breath control, is a cornerstone of yoga. By cultivating awareness of the breath, individuals connect with the present moment, calm the mind, and enhance the flow of vital energy (prana) throughout the body.

Meditation and Mindfulness (Dhyana):

- The practice of meditation, or Dhyana, deepens the journey inward. Through mindfulness and focused attention, individuals explore the landscape of the mind, transcending the fluctuations of thoughts and emotions to discover a reservoir of inner peace.

Ethical Guidelines (Yamas and Niyamas):

- The Yamas and Niyamas, ethical principles that guide personal and social conduct, provide a moral foundation for yoga practice. Cultivating qualities such as compassion, truthfulness, contentment, and self-discipline creates a harmonious and peaceful way of living.

Devotion and Surrender (Bhakti Yoga):

- Bhakti Yoga, the path of devotion, invites individuals to cultivate a heart-centered approach to practice. By surrendering to a higher purpose or divine presence, practitioners find solace and a source of enduring peace.

Yoga for Peace: The Physical Manifestation

In the physical realm of yoga, specific poses are designed to foster relaxation, release tension, and invite a sense of calm. The following selection of yoga poses serves as a repertoire for cultivating peace, both within the body and the mind:

Child's Pose (Balasana):

- A gentle, resting pose, Child's Pose invites individuals to kneel on the mat with the forehead resting on the ground, arms extended or resting alongside the body. This pose provides a sense of surrender, releasing tension from the back, shoulders, and hips, while encouraging introspection and relaxation.

Easy Pose (Sukhasana):

- Seated comfortably with crossed legs, Easy Pose allows individuals to ground themselves and find a sense of stability. This foundational pose is conducive to meditation and breath awareness, fostering a tranquil state of mind.

Corpse Pose (Savasana):

- The ultimate relaxation pose, Corpse Pose involves lying flat on the back with arms and legs extended. Savasana invites a conscious release of muscular tension, promoting deep relaxation and a meditative state. It symbolizes the surrender of the ego, leading to a profound sense of peace.

Legs Up the Wall (Viparita Karani):

- A gentle inversion, Legs Up the Wall involves lying on the back with legs extended vertically against a wall. This pose encourages relaxation, relieves tension in the legs, and promotes a gentle flow of energy throughout the body. Viparita Karani is known for its calming effects on the nervous system.

Seated Forward Bend (Paschimottanasana):

- Seated Forward Bend involves extending the legs in front and folding forward from the hips. This pose stretches the spine, hamstrings, and lower back, while also calming the mind. The forward folding motion encourages introspection and a sense of surrender.

Reclining Bound Angle Pose (Supta Baddha Konasana):

- In this restorative pose, the soles of the feet come together as the knees open outward, creating a diamond shape with the legs. Lying back with support under the spine, individuals experience a gentle opening of the hips and chest, promoting a sense of ease and peace.

Cat-Cow Stretch (Marjaryasana-Bitilasana):

- The dynamic flow between Cat and Cow poses involves arching and rounding the spine in a coordinated movement with the breath. This gentle flow promotes spinal flexibility, releases tension in the back, and encourages a mindful connection between movement and breath.

Tree Pose (Vrksasana):

- A balancing pose, Tree Pose invites individuals to stand on one leg while placing the sole of the other foot on the inner thigh or calf. This pose cultivates balance, focus, and a sense of rootedness, creating a serene foundation for the mind.

Bridge Pose (Setu Bandhasana):

- Bridge Pose involves lying on the back, lifting the hips toward the sky, and interlacing the hands under the body. This pose opens the chest, strengthens the legs, and provides an invigorating stretch for the spine. The backbend element energizes the body while instilling a sense of openness and vitality.

Supported Shoulderstand (Salamba Sarvangasana):

- In Supported Shoulderstand, the body is inverted, with the legs extended overhead and supported by the hands on the lower back. This pose stimulates the thyroid gland, promotes circulation, and induces a calming effect on the nervous system, fostering a sense of tranquility.

The Flow of Peace: Creating a Sequence

To weave these poses into a harmonious sequence, consider the following flow designed to cultivate peace, mindfulness, and relaxation:

1. Centering (Easy Pose):

- Begin in a comfortable seated position, grounding yourself with focused breath awareness. Allow the breath to become a gentle anchor, drawing your attention inward.

2. Gentle Warm-Up (Cat-Cow Stretch):
- Transition into a gentle Cat-Cow flow to warm up the spine and invite movement into the body. Coordinate each movement with the breath, fostering a mindful connection.

3. Grounding and Stability (Tree Pose):
- Shift into Tree Pose, finding stability on one leg and extending the other foot to create a sense of balance and rootedness. Engage the breath to center the mind.

4. Opening and Release (Reclining Bound Angle Pose):
- Transition to the floor for Reclining Bound Angle Pose. With support under the spine, allow the hips to gently open, creating a sense of release and ease.

5. Dynamic Movement (Bridge Pose):
- Flow into Bridge Pose to energize the body and stimulate the spine. Feel the lift of the hips, engaging the legs and opening the chest for a revitalizing stretch.

6. Inversion and Calm (Supported Shoulderstand):
- Move into Supported Shoulderstand, allowing the inversion to bring a sense of calm. Support the lower back with the hands and feel the gentle stretch in the neck and shoulders.

7. Surrender and Introspection (Child's Pose):
- Ease into Child's Pose, surrendering the body to the mat. This pose invites introspection and a sense of letting go.

8. Deep Relaxation (Corpse Pose):

- Conclude the sequence with Corpse Pose, extending the legs and arms in a position of total relaxation. Allow the body and mind to absorb the benefits of the practice.

Cultivating Mindfulness in Yoga Practice

Beyond the physical postures, mindfulness is a key element in harnessing the full transformative power of yoga. Consider incorporating the following mindfulness practices into your yoga sessions for enhanced peace and presence:

Conscious Breath Awareness:

- Throughout your practice, maintain awareness of the breath. Notice the inhales and exhales, allowing the breath to guide the rhythm of movement. This conscious breath awareness deepens the connection between the body and mind.

Gentle Transitions:

- Transition between poses with mindfulness and intention. Instead of rushing, move with awareness, feeling each movement and the sensations it brings. The spaces between poses offer opportunities for reflection and mindful presence.

Body Scan Meditation:

- Integrate a body scan meditation into your practice. As you move through each pose, bring attention to different parts of the body, releasing tension and cultivating a sense of presence in the moment.

Focused Affirmations:

- Incorporate positive affirmations or intentions into your practice. As you hold each pose, silently repeat affirmations that resonate with a sense of peace, such as "I am calm," "I am grounded," or "I am at ease."

Gratitude Reflection:

- During moments of stillness, take a moment for gratitude reflection. Acknowledge the sensations, the breath, and the opportunity to practice. Cultivating gratitude enhances the overall sense of peace and contentment.

Case Studies: The Transformative Journey Within

Case Study 1: Emma's Path to Inner Calm

Background: Emma, a busy professional, struggled with stress and insomnia.

Yoga Practice Intervention:

- Evening Yoga Sequence: Emma incorporated a gentle evening yoga sequence into her routine, focusing on restorative poses and calming breathwork.

Outcomes:

- Improved Sleep Quality: Over time, Emma experienced improved sleep quality. The evening yoga practice served as a powerful tool for unwinding, releasing tension, and creating a peaceful transition from the demands of the day to a restful night.

Case Study 2: Michael's Journey to Mindful Living

Background: Michael, a student, faced challenges with focus and overwhelm.

Yoga Practice Intervention:

- Morning Mindfulness Flow: Michael established a morning routine incorporating mindful yoga poses, breathwork, and short meditations to set a positive tone for the day.

Outcomes:

- Enhanced Focus and Clarity: The morning mindfulness flow became a cornerstone of Michael's day. He reported enhanced focus, mental clarity, and an increased ability to navigate academic challenges with a sense of calm and resilience.

The Yoga of Everyday Life: Integrating Peaceful Presence

As we carry the essence of yoga off the mat and into the tapestry of everyday life, let the practice become a lived experience—a continuous journey of mindful presence and inner peace. Consider the following ways to integrate the principles of yoga into daily living:

Mindful Breathing Breaks:

- Incorporate brief mindful breathing breaks throughout the day. Whether at work, in transit, or during moments of stress, pause to take a few conscious breaths, centering yourself in the present moment.

Mindful Walking:

- Transform walking into a mindfulness practice. As you walk, pay attention to each step, the sensations in your feet, and the rhythm of your breath. This simple act of walking becomes a moving meditation, fostering peace and awareness.

Mindful Eating:

- Bring mindfulness to your meals. Slow down, savor each bite, and notice the flavors, textures, and nourishment of the food. Eating with awareness not only enhances digestion but also cultivates a sense of gratitude for the sustenance received.

Mindful Communication:

- Infuse mindfulness into your interactions with others. Practice active listening, offering your full attention without judgment. Approach conversations with a sense of compassion and understanding, fostering harmonious relationships.

Mindful Technology Use:

- Consciously engage with technology. Set boundaries for screen time, create tech-free zones, and practice digital detoxes. Mindful technology use promotes a healthier balance and prevents the intrusion of constant stimuli into moments of peace.

Conclusion: A Mat of Infinite Peace

In the gentle embrace of yoga poses for peace, may every stretch, every breath, and every moment on the mat be a stepping stone into the sanctuary of inner calm. As we conclude our exploration of yoga's transformative potential, let the wisdom of the practice linger—a timeless reminder that peace is not a destination but a continuous journey, woven into the fabric of our existence.

May the practice of yoga extend beyond the mat—a living, breathing expression of mindful presence, serenity, and the boundless peace that resides within. As we transition to the subsequent chapters, may the echoes of yoga's ancient wisdom reverberate—a call to cultivate peace not only in the sanctuary of practice but in every step of the journey called life.

Dance Therapy

In the rhythmic language of movement, dance emerges as a universal expression of joy, liberation, and emotional release. Beyond its cultural and social dimensions, dance holds therapeutic potential, offering a unique pathway to fuel positivity and enhance well-being. In this exploration, we delve into the realm of dance therapy—a dynamic and transformative practice that harnesses the power of movement to cultivate positivity, emotional resilience, and a profound sense of self-expression. As we step onto the dance floor, let the music guide us on a journey of discovery, healing, and the boundless potential of movement as a catalyst for positive transformation.

The Essence of Dance Therapy

A Dance of Healing: Dance therapy, also known as dance/movement therapy (DMT), is a holistic and expressive form of psychotherapy that integrates movement, dance, and creative expression to promote emotional, cognitive, and physical well-being. Rooted in the belief that the body and mind are interconnected, dance therapy recognizes the body as a vessel for communication, self-discovery, and healing.

The Language of the Body: In dance therapy, the body becomes a metaphorical canvas, and movement becomes the language through which individuals communicate and explore their inner worlds. The non-verbal nature of this therapeutic modality allows for the expression of emotions, memories, and experiences that may be challenging to articulate verbally.

Integration of Mind and Body: Dance therapy goes beyond the confines of traditional talk therapy by actively engaging the body in the therapeutic process. Through intentional movement, individuals have the opportunity to integrate thoughts, emotions, and physical sensations, fostering a deeper connection between mind and body.

Creativity and Self-Expression: One of the hallmarks of dance therapy is its emphasis on creativity and self-expression. The dance floor becomes a safe and non-judgmental space for individuals to explore and express their authentic selves, transcending societal expectations and limitations.

Adaptability and Inclusivity: Dance therapy is inherently adaptable and inclusive. It can be tailored to accommodate individuals of all ages, abilities, and backgrounds. Whether in one-on-one sessions, group settings, or community programs, dance therapy offers a versatile and accessible approach to fostering positive transformation.

The Therapeutic Benefits of Dance

Emotional Release and Catharsis: Dance therapy provides a cathartic outlet for the expression of emotions. Through movement, individuals can release pent-up feelings, process grief, and navigate the complexities of their emotional landscapes. The rhythmic flow of dance becomes a vehicle for emotional release and a catalyst for healing.

Stress Reduction and Relaxation: Engaging in dance promotes relaxation and stress reduction. The rhythmic and repetitive nature of movement activates the parasympathetic nervous system, leading to a state of calm and relaxation. As individuals immerse themselves in the dance, tension dissipates, and a sense of ease prevails.

Body Awareness and Mindfulness: Dance therapy cultivates body awareness and mindfulness. Through intentional movement, individuals become attuned to physical sensations, gaining insight into the mind-body connection. This heightened awareness fosters mindfulness, promoting a present-centered experience on the dance floor.

Enhanced Self-Esteem and Body Image: The positive embodiment experienced in dance therapy contributes to enhanced self-esteem and a positive body image. As individuals celebrate their bodies' capabilities and expressiveness, they develop a more compassionate and accepting relationship with themselves.

Improved Mental Health: Dance therapy is recognized for its positive impact on mental health. Research indicates that engaging in dance can reduce symptoms of anxiety, depression, and stress. The combination of movement, creative expression, and the release of endorphins contributes to an overall sense of well-being.

Social Connection and Community Building: In group dance therapy settings, individuals experience a sense of social connection and community. The shared experience of movement fosters a sense of belonging, reduces feelings of isolation, and creates a supportive environment for personal growth.

Dance Styles and Therapeutic Applications

Freeform and Improvisational Dance: Freeform and improvisational dance provide individuals with the freedom to move spontaneously and expressively. This style allows for a direct and unfiltered connection with one's emotions, fostering authentic self-expression and creativity.

Improvisational dance is particularly effective for those who may feel inhibited or restricted in more structured forms of movement.

Expressive Dance: Expressive dance involves intentionally conveying emotions and thoughts through movement. Individuals explore specific themes, memories, or experiences using various dance elements such as gesture, shape, and dynamics. Expressive dance allows for the externalization of internal processes, providing a therapeutic outlet for self-discovery.

Therapeutic Dance/Movement Programs: Structured dance/movement programs designed for therapeutic purposes are implemented in various settings. These programs may include specific themes or objectives, such as stress reduction, trauma recovery, or enhancing emotional intelligence. Trained dance/movement therapists guide participants through sequences and exercises tailored to therapeutic goals.

Dance for Embodiment and Mindfulness: Certain dance practices focus on embodiment and mindfulness, emphasizing the conscious awareness of bodily sensations and movements. Participants engage in slow, deliberate movements, heightening their sensitivity to the present moment. This approach is particularly beneficial for promoting mindfulness and relaxation.

Ecstatic Dance: Ecstatic dance is a contemporary form of freeform movement that encourages uninhibited self-expression. Participants engage in spontaneous and often energetic dance, guided by music that spans various genres. Ecstatic dance events provide a communal and liberating space for individuals to connect with their bodies and express themselves freely.

Dance Therapy in Practice: Case Studies

Case Study 1: Sarah's Journey to Emotional Release

Background: Sarah, a survivor of trauma, struggled with processing and expressing her emotions.

Dance Therapy Intervention:

- Improvisational Dance Sessions: Sarah participated in improvisational dance sessions, guided by a dance therapist. These sessions provided a safe space for Sarah to explore her emotions, release pent-up tension, and gradually reconnect with her body.

Outcomes:

- Emotional Release: Over time, Sarah experienced a significant release of emotions through movement. Improvisational dance allowed her to express and process feelings that were challenging to verbalize. The therapeutic dance sessions became a pivotal aspect of her healing journey.

Case Study 2: James' Exploration of Self-Expression

Background: James, a teenager struggling with self-esteem issues, found it difficult to express himself verbally.

Dance Therapy Intervention:

- Expressive Dance Program: James participated in an expressive dance program specifically designed for teenagers. Through guided exercises and thematic dance sessions, he explored his emotions and thoughts using movement as a form of communication.

Outcomes:

- Enhanced Self-Esteem: James developed enhanced self-esteem and a more positive body image through expressive dance. The program provided him with a platform to express himself creatively, fostering a sense of empowerment and self-acceptance.

Facilitating Dance Therapy: Principles and Considerations

Creating a Safe Space: Establishing a safe and non-judgmental environment is paramount in dance therapy. Therapists ensure that participants feel secure and supported, emphasizing consent and the freedom to choose the level of engagement. This safe space encourages authentic self-expression and vulnerability.

Cultivating Mindfulness: Dance therapy incorporates mindfulness principles, encouraging participants to stay present in the moment. Mindful movement involves paying attention to bodily sensations, emotions, and the quality of movement. Cultivating mindfulness in dance enhances the therapeutic benefits of the practice.

Adaptability and Inclusivity: Dance therapy sessions are adaptable to accommodate diverse individuals and groups. Considerations such as physical abilities, cultural background, and personal preferences are taken into account to ensure an inclusive and accessible experience for all participants.

Integrating Verbal Processing: While dance therapy is primarily non-verbal, there is space for verbal processing if and when participants choose to articulate their experiences. Therapists may integrate moments of reflection or discussion to complement the non-verbal exploration, allowing individuals to integrate their movement experiences into words.

Building Trust and Connection: Building a trusting therapeutic relationship is foundational in dance therapy. Therapists foster trust through empathy, attunement, and a deep understanding of each individual's unique journey. This trust creates a foundation for participants to engage authentically in the therapeutic process.

Music Selection and Atmosphere: The choice of music plays a crucial role in dance therapy. Therapists select music that aligns with the therapeutic goals, evokes emotions, and supports the overall atmosphere of the session. The rhythmic qualities and emotional resonance of the music enhance the transformative potential of the dance experience.

Conclusion: Dancing into Positivity

In the tapestry of therapeutic modalities, dance therapy stands as a vibrant thread—a testament to the profound connection between movement, emotion, and well-being. As we conclude our exploration of dance therapy, let the rhythm of possibility linger—a reminder that the dance floor is a canvas for personal transformation, healing, and the joyful celebration of life.

May the dance of therapy continue—an ever-evolving expression of resilience, self-discovery, and the innate positivity that arises when we move to the beat of our authentic selves. As we transition to the subsequent chapters, may the spirit of dance resonate—an invitation to step into the transformative embrace of movement, where every step is a dance of empowerment and every movement is a gesture of profound self-expression.

Laughter as Powerful Medicine

In the symphony of human experience, laughter emerges as a universal language, transcending cultural boundaries and connecting individuals in moments of joy. Beyond its role as a spontaneous expression of mirth, laughter is recognized as a potent force for healing and well-being. In this exploration, we delve into the therapeutic realm of laughter—a practice that harnesses the transformative power of humor and merriment to fuel positivity, reduce stress, and cultivate a profound sense of joy. As we embark on this journey, let the laughter ripple through the pages, reminding us of the innate and contagious nature of mirthful moments.

The Science of Laughter

The Neurochemistry of Joy: Laughter is more than a delightful sound—it's a neurochemical symphony that unfolds in the brain, releasing a cascade of feel-good neurotransmitters. The act of laughter triggers the release of endorphins, the body's natural painkillers, promoting a sense of euphoria and well-being. Additionally, laughter enhances the production of dopamine, a neurotransmitter associated with reward and pleasure.

Stress Reduction and Cortisol Regulation: Laughter serves as a natural stress buster, influencing the body's stress response system. The act of laughing reduces the levels of cortisol, a stress hormone, leading to a state of relaxation. The rhythmic muscle contractions involved in laughter also promote physical release, alleviating tension and creating a sense of ease.

Cardiovascular Benefits: The cardiovascular system receives a dose of well-being through laughter. Laughter increases blood flow and improves blood vessel function, contributing to better cardiovascular health. The relaxation response triggered by laughter is associated with lower blood pressure, potentially reducing the risk of cardiovascular diseases.

Immune System Enhancement: Laughter is a boost for the immune system. The release of neuropeptides, small proteins that help regulate the immune system, is stimulated by laughter. This immune response, combined with the overall reduction in stress, contributes to a more robust defense against illnesses.

Abdominal Workout: In the realm of physical exercise, laughter is a delightful surprise. The act of laughing engages various muscles, especially those in the abdomen. A hearty laugh can be likened to a mini workout, toning abdominal muscles and providing a subtle form of exercise.

Laughter Yoga: Blending Movement and Joy

The Birth of Laughter Yoga: Laughter Yoga, a unique and innovative practice, combines laughter exercises with yogic deep-breathing techniques. Founded by Dr. Madan Kataria in 1995, Laughter Yoga originated in a park in Mumbai, India, as a small group engaged in laughter to promote well-being. Today, Laughter Yoga has evolved into a global phenomenon, with laughter clubs in numerous countries.

Laughter Yoga Exercises: Laughter Yoga sessions involve a series of intentional laughter exercises, often accompanied by playful activities and group dynamics.

Participants engage in spontaneous laughter, guided laughter, and imaginative play to evoke genuine and contagious laughter. Laughter Yoga sessions typically conclude with laughter meditation and relaxation.

The Joyful Impact: The benefits of Laughter Yoga extend beyond the physiological effects of laughter. The practice fosters a sense of playfulness, social connection, and a childlike spirit. Laughter Yoga emphasizes the philosophy of "laugh for no reason," highlighting that laughter can be cultivated as a choice, independent of external circumstances.

Laughter Clubs Worldwide: Laughter Yoga has inspired the establishment of laughter clubs around the world. In laughter clubs, individuals gather regularly to engage in laughter exercises, share joyous moments, and experience the collective upliftment that laughter brings. Laughter clubs promote a sense of community, support, and the shared pursuit of well-being.

The Therapeutic Role of Humor

Humor as a Coping Mechanism: Humor serves as a powerful coping mechanism in the face of adversity. The ability to find humor in challenging situations is associated with increased resilience and a more optimistic outlook. Humor provides a cognitive shift, allowing individuals to reframe their perspectives and navigate difficulties with a lighthearted approach.

Social Bonding Through Humor: Laughter is a social glue, fostering connections and strengthening relationships. Shared laughter creates a sense of camaraderie and mutual understanding. Humor serves as a language of connection, transcending verbal communication and bringing people together in moments of shared merriment.

Cultural and Therapeutic Humor: The therapeutic use of humor, often referred to as therapeutic humor or laughter therapy, integrates humor into the healing process. Therapists may employ humor as a tool to alleviate stress, enhance communication, and create a positive therapeutic environment. Humor is recognized as a valuable aspect of holistic well-being.

Incorporating Laughter and Movement

Laughter Exercises for Positivity: Incorporating laughter exercises into daily life can be a simple yet impactful way to enhance positivity. These exercises may include laughter stretches, imaginary laughter, and laughter affirmations. Engaging in intentional laughter, even for a few minutes each day, contributes to the overall well-being.

Dance of Joy: Combining laughter with movement amplifies its positive effects. Consider integrating dance and laughter into joyful sessions. Whether through spontaneous dance parties, laughter yoga with dance elements, or laughter-infused movement meditations, the fusion of laughter and dance creates a harmonious celebration of life.

Laughter Meditation: Laughter meditation involves a blend of deep-breathing techniques, intentional laughter, and moments of stillness. Participants engage in laughter followed by moments of silent meditation, allowing the joyful energy of laughter to permeate the mind and body. Laughter meditation promotes relaxation and a heightened state of mindfulness.

Laughter Retreats and Events: Participating in laughter retreats or events offers an immersive experience of laughter and movement. These gatherings often include a combination of laughter exercises, dance, and expressive activities. Laughter retreats provide an opportunity to connect with like-minded individuals, share laughter, and explore the transformative power of joy.

Laughter and Positive Psychology

Positive Psychology Perspective: Laughter aligns with the principles of positive psychology—a field that focuses on the strengths and virtues that contribute to a fulfilling life. Positive psychology emphasizes the importance of positive emotions, engagement, relationships, meaning, and accomplishments. Laughter, as a positive emotion, plays a central role in promoting overall well-being.

The Broadening and Building Theory: According to the Broadening and Building Theory proposed by psychologist Barbara Fredrickson, positive emotions, including laughter, broaden individuals' thought-action repertoires and build lasting personal resources. Laughter, as a positive emotion, opens individuals to new possibilities, fosters creativity, and enhances resilience.

Laughter and Emotional Intelligence: Laughter is a key aspect of emotional intelligence, contributing to self-awareness, social awareness, and interpersonal relationships. The ability to navigate and express emotions through humor enhances emotional resilience and cultivates a positive social environment.

Humor in the Workplace: The integration of humor and laughter in the workplace has become recognized for its positive impact on employee well-being and productivity. Humor in the workplace contributes to a positive organizational culture, fosters teamwork, and serves as a coping mechanism in high-stress environments.

The Healing Power of Laughter: Case Studies

Case Study 1: Emily's Journey to Stress Reduction

Background: Emily, a working professional, faced high levels of stress and burnout.

Laughter Therapy Intervention:

- Daily Laughter Exercises: Emily incorporated daily laughter exercises into her routine. These exercises included intentional laughter, humor appreciation, and laughter meditation. Emily also attended laughter yoga sessions to experience the collective joy of laughter.

Outcomes:

- Stress Reduction: Over time, Emily reported a significant reduction in stress levels. The regular practice of laughter exercises provided her with a practical and enjoyable tool for managing stress. Emily's overall well-being improved, and she felt more resilient in the face of workplace challenges.

Case Study 2: Jake's Exploration of Social Connection

Background: Jake, a retiree, experienced feelings of isolation and loneliness.

Laughter Club Participation:

- Joining a Laughter Club: Seeking social connection, Jake joined a local laughter club. The laughter club provided a supportive community where individuals engaged in laughter exercises, shared jokes, and celebrated moments of joy together.

Outcomes:

- Improved Social Well-Being: Through laughter club participation, Jake experienced a renewed sense of social well-being. The shared laughter created bonds with club members, reducing feelings of isolation. Jake's participation in laughter club activities became a highlight of his week, contributing to a more joyful retirement.

Facilitating Laughter and Positive Practices

Creating a Laughter Routine: Establishing a laughter routine involves incorporating intentional laughter exercises into daily life. This may include laughter breaks, humor appreciation moments, or joining laughter groups. Creating a laughter routine cultivates a habit of joy, contributing to a positive and resilient mindset.

Laughter and Mindfulness: Mindful laughter involves being fully present in the moment while engaging in laughter. Mindful laughter practices may include paying attention to the sensations of laughter, the breath, and the overall experience. Combining mindfulness with laughter enhances the therapeutic benefits of both practices.

Laughter in Social Settings: Fostering laughter in social settings contributes to positive group dynamics and relationship building. Encourage laughter-sharing moments, humor appreciation sessions, or team-building activities that incorporate humor. Laughter creates a shared language that strengthens social bonds.

Laughter Wellness Programs: Organizations may consider implementing laughter wellness programs to promote employee well-being. These programs can include laughter yoga sessions, humor workshops, and laughter-infused team-building activities. Laughter wellness programs contribute to a positive workplace culture and support employees in managing stress.

Humor and Resilience Workshops: Workshops that focus on humor and resilience provide individuals with tools to navigate challenges with a positive mindset. These workshops may include humor exploration, resilience-building exercises, and strategies for incorporating humor into daily life. Humor and resilience workshops empower individuals to face adversity with grace and humor.

Conclusion: The Symphony of Laughter

As we conclude our exploration of laughter as a powerful medicine, let the echoes of joy reverberate in our hearts—a reminder that laughter is an elixir of life, a source of healing, and a bridge to a brighter and more resilient existence.

May the laughter continue—a timeless melody that uplifts, connects, and transcends the boundaries of circumstance. As we transition to the subsequent chapters, may the spirit of laughter linger—an invitation to dance with joy, to share in the laughter of others, and to savor the profound medicine that resides in the simple act of laughter.

Chapter 5: Healthy Eating for Clarity
Nutrients for Well-Being

In the intricate dance of well-being, the role of nutrition is akin to a choreographer, orchestrating a symphony of essential elements that nourish the body and mind. As we embark on the exploration of healthy eating for clarity, our focus shifts to the pivotal role of nutrients—the building blocks of vitality and cognitive function. Within this nutritional realm, we uncover the profound impact of specific nutrients on overall well-being, mental clarity, and the cultivation of a vibrant and balanced life.

The Foundation of Nutrient-Rich Eating

Essential Nutrients: At the core of nutrient-rich eating are essential nutrients—substances that the body requires for proper functioning but cannot produce in sufficient quantities. These include vitamins, minerals, amino acids, fatty acids, and carbohydrates. A well-balanced diet that encompasses a variety of nutrient-rich foods ensures the intake of these essential elements.

Macronutrients: Macronutrients are nutrients that the body needs in relatively large amounts. These include carbohydrates, proteins, and fats. Each macronutrient plays a distinct role in supporting bodily functions. Carbohydrates provide energy, proteins are essential for tissue repair and growth, and fats are crucial for cell structure and nutrient absorption.

Micronutrients: Micronutrients are nutrients required in smaller quantities but are equally vital for health. This category includes vitamins and minerals. Vitamins are organic compounds that support various physiological processes, while minerals are inorganic elements essential for functions such as bone health, nerve transmission, and fluid balance.

Nutrients and Cognitive Function

Omega-3 Fatty Acids: Omega-3 fatty acids, particularly eicosapentaenoic acid (EPA) and docosahexaenoic acid (DHA), are crucial for brain health. These fatty acids contribute to the structure of cell membranes in the brain and possess anti-inflammatory properties. Fatty fish, flaxseeds, chia seeds, and walnuts are excellent sources of omega-3 fatty acids.

Antioxidants: Antioxidants play a protective role in the brain by neutralizing free radicals, which are molecules that can cause oxidative stress and damage cells. Rich sources of antioxidants include fruits (such as berries, citrus fruits, and apples), vegetables (such as spinach, kale, and carrots), and nuts (such as almonds and hazelnuts).

Vitamins B and C: B vitamins, particularly B6, B9 (folate), and B12, play a crucial role in cognitive function. They are involved in the synthesis of neurotransmitters, the chemicals that transmit signals in the brain. Foods rich in B vitamins include leafy greens, legumes, whole grains, and lean meats. Vitamin C, found in fruits and vegetables like oranges, strawberries, and bell peppers, is also important for brain health and acts as an antioxidant.

Iron: Iron is essential for transporting oxygen to the brain. An adequate supply of oxygen is crucial for cognitive function and concentration. Foods rich in iron include lean meats, poultry, fish, legumes, and iron-fortified cereals.

Zinc: Zinc plays a role in neurotransmitter function and can impact mood and cognitive performance. Foods rich in zinc include meat, dairy products, nuts, and legumes.

Nutrient-Dense Foods for Cognitive Clarity

Blueberries: Blueberries are often referred to as "brain berries" due to their rich content of antioxidants, particularly anthocyanins. These compounds have been linked to improvements in cognitive function, including memory and learning.

Broccoli: Broccoli is a nutrient powerhouse, providing a high concentration of vitamin K, which is essential for forming sphingolipids, a type of fat densely packed into brain cells. It also contains antioxidants and is a good source of folate.

Dark Chocolate: Dark chocolate, in moderation, can be a delightful addition to a brain-boosting diet. It contains flavonoids, caffeine, and antioxidants that may enhance memory and mood. Choose dark chocolate with at least 70% cocoa content for maximum benefits.

Nuts and Seeds: Nuts and seeds, such as almonds, walnuts, flaxseeds, and chia seeds, are rich in omega-3 fatty acids, antioxidants, and vitamin E. These nutrients contribute to overall brain health and may support cognitive function.

Eggs: Eggs are a source of several nutrients beneficial for the brain, including choline, which is a precursor to acetylcholine, a neurotransmitter involved in mood and memory regulation. Eggs also provide high-quality proteins and B vitamins.

Leafy Greens: Leafy greens like spinach, kale, and Swiss chard are rich in vitamins, minerals, and antioxidants. They provide a variety of nutrients, including folate, vitamin K, and lutein, which are associated with cognitive health.

Nutrient Synergy and Whole Foods

The Power of Nutrient Synergy: Whole foods contain a combination of nutrients that often work synergistically, enhancing their collective benefits. For example, the combination of vitamin C and iron in a spinach and strawberry salad promotes better iron absorption. Emphasizing a variety of nutrient-dense whole foods ensures a holistic approach to well-being.

The Mediterranean Diet: The Mediterranean diet, characterized by an abundance of fruits, vegetables, whole grains, nuts, seeds, and olive oil, is often hailed for its positive impact on cognitive health. Rich in antioxidants, omega-3 fatty acids, and vitamins, this diet has been associated with a lower risk of cognitive decline.

Mindful Eating Practices: Practicing mindful eating involves paying attention to the sensory experience of eating, including taste, texture, and aroma. Mindful eating encourages a conscious connection with food, fostering a more profound appreciation for the nourishment it provides. This approach contributes to a balanced and positive relationship with food.

Nutritional Strategies for Cognitive Clarity

Balancing Macronutrients: A well-balanced intake of carbohydrates, proteins, and fats is essential for sustained energy levels and cognitive function. Including whole grains, lean proteins, and healthy fats in meals supports a steady release of energy and mental clarity throughout the day.

Hydration for Cognitive Function: Staying adequately hydrated is crucial for cognitive function. Dehydration can lead to difficulties in concentration, fatigue, and a decline in overall cognitive performance. Consuming water, herbal teas, and hydrating foods (such as water-rich fruits and vegetables) supports optimal brain function.

Moderating Sugar Intake: While glucose is a primary source of energy for the brain, excessive sugar intake can lead to fluctuations in blood sugar levels, affecting mood and cognitive function. Choosing complex carbohydrates, such as whole grains, and moderating added sugar intake contribute to stable energy levels.

Incorporating Functional Foods: Functional foods are those that provide health benefits beyond basic nutrition. Including functional foods, such as turmeric (containing curcumin with anti-inflammatory properties) and green tea (rich in antioxidants and L-theanine), can contribute to cognitive well-being.

Mindful Eating Practices for Clarity

Savoring Each Bite: Mindful eating involves savoring each bite, paying attention to flavors, textures, and aromas. Taking the time to appreciate the sensory experience of eating enhances the enjoyment of meals and promotes a positive relationship with food.

Eating with Awareness: Eating with awareness involves being present in the moment while consuming meals. Minimize distractions, such as electronic devices, and focus on the act of eating. This practice supports mindful decision-making regarding food choices and portion sizes.

Recognizing Hunger and Fullness Cues: Tuning in to hunger and fullness cues helps regulate food intake. Mindful eating involves recognizing physical hunger and satiety signals, allowing for a more intuitive and balanced approach to eating.

Appreciating Nutrient-Rich Foods: Expressing gratitude for the nourishment provided by nutrient-rich foods is a mindful practice. Cultivating an appreciation for the vitality and clarity that these foods contribute encourages a positive and intentional approach to eating.

Culinary Exploration and Well-Being

The Joy of Cooking: Engaging in culinary exploration can be a source of joy and well-being. Experimenting with new recipes, flavors, and cooking techniques adds variety to meals and enhances the overall dining experience. The process of preparing nourishing meals contributes to a sense of accomplishment and connection with food.

Cultural Diversity in Cuisine: Exploring diverse cuisines allows for a rich tapestry of nutrient-rich foods. Different cultures offer a vast array of flavors, ingredients, and culinary traditions. Embracing cultural diversity in cuisine not only expands the palate but also provides a diverse range of nutrients.

Mindful Meal Planning: Planning meals mindfully involves considering nutritional needs, variety, and personal preferences. Mindful meal planning supports the creation of balanced and satisfying meals, promoting both physical and mental well-being.

Conclusion: Nourishing the Mind and Body

As we conclude our exploration of nutrients for well-being, let the essence of nourishment linger—a reminder that the foods we choose are not merely sustenance but a profound source of vitality, clarity, and holistic well-being.

May the journey of nutrient-rich eating be a celebration—a symphony of flavors, colors, and textures that harmonize to support cognitive clarity, physical vitality, and the cultivation of a vibrant life. As we transition to the subsequent chapters, may the spirit of mindful nourishment resonate—an invitation to savor each bite, appreciate the richness of whole foods, and embrace the nourishing dance of well-being.

Traditional Foods for Grounding

In the journey toward clarity and well-being, the exploration of healthy eating extends beyond nutritional content to embrace the wisdom of traditional foods. Traditional cuisines, rooted in cultural practices and ancestral knowledge, offer a unique tapestry of flavors and nourishment that extends beyond the physical to encompass a sense of grounding. In this chapter, we delve into the significance of traditional foods, their role in fostering a connection to heritage, and the impact of these culinary traditions on overall well-being.

The Essence of Traditional Foods

Cultural Significance: Traditional foods hold profound cultural significance, acting as carriers of heritage, history, and identity. Passed down through generations, these culinary traditions become a tangible link to the past, offering a sense of continuity and connection to one's cultural roots. Embracing traditional foods is not merely a culinary choice but a celebration of cultural richness.

Harmony with Nature: Many traditional diets are inherently aligned with the natural environment. Traditional societies often developed their culinary practices based on local and seasonal ingredients. This harmony with nature not only promotes sustainability but also ensures that the nutritional content of foods is attuned to the needs of the community within a specific geographical region.

Balanced Nutrition: Traditional diets, crafted over centuries, often reflect a deep understanding of balanced nutrition. These diets typically incorporate a variety of foods from different food groups, providing essential nutrients in proportions that support overall health. Traditional cuisines offer a holistic approach to nourishment, considering not only individual nutrients but also their synergistic interactions.

Embracing Heritage Through Traditional Foods

Culinary Rituals: Traditional foods are often intertwined with culinary rituals that extend beyond the act of eating. These rituals may include special preparation methods, communal cooking practices, or the observance of specific customs during meals. Engaging in these culinary rituals fosters a sense of mindfulness, gratitude, and connection to the cultural roots embedded in each dish.

Festive Celebrations: Many traditional foods are central to festive celebrations and cultural ceremonies. These occasions not only mark significant milestones but also serve as opportunities for communities to come together, share in the preparation and enjoyment of traditional dishes, and reinforce a collective sense of identity and belonging.

Seasonal Wisdom: Traditional cuisines often place emphasis on seasonal eating, recognizing the cyclical nature of agriculture and the availability of specific foods throughout the year. Seasonal eating not only ensures the freshness and nutritional quality of ingredients but also aligns with the natural rhythms of the environment.

Traditional Foods and Emotional Well-Being

Comfort and Familiarity: Traditional foods often evoke a sense of comfort and familiarity, creating a connection to emotional well-being. The flavors, aromas, and textures of dishes prepared in accordance with cultural traditions have the power to evoke memories, provide a sense of security, and offer emotional nourishment.

Culinary Heritage as a Source of Resilience: In times of challenge or upheaval, turning to traditional foods can serve as a source of resilience. The act of preparing and consuming familiar dishes provides a grounding anchor, offering a sense of stability and continuity amid change. Culinary heritage becomes a tool for navigating life's uncertainties.

Shared Stories and Wisdom: Traditional foods are carriers of stories, wisdom, and collective experiences. The process of learning traditional recipes, understanding their cultural significance, and passing this knowledge to future generations fosters a sense of continuity and shared identity. Traditional foods become vessels for the transmission of cultural narratives and values.

Examples of Traditional Foods for Grounding

Mediterranean Diet: The Mediterranean diet, rooted in the culinary traditions of countries bordering the Mediterranean Sea, is renowned for its health benefits and grounding qualities. Rich in fruits, vegetables, whole grains, olive oil, and lean proteins, this diet emphasizes balance, moderation, and the enjoyment of meals in a communal setting.

Japanese Washoku: Washoku, the traditional Japanese cuisine, is characterized by its emphasis on seasonal and locally sourced ingredients. Centered around rice, vegetables, fish, and pickled items, Washoku embodies the principles of balance, harmony, and respect for nature.

The ritualistic preparation and presentation of Washoku contribute to its grounding effect.

Indian Ayurvedic Cuisine: Ayurvedic cuisine, rooted in the ancient Indian system of medicine, emphasizes the balance of doshas (fundamental energies) to promote holistic well-being. Incorporating a variety of herbs, spices, grains, legumes, and seasonal vegetables, Ayurvedic cuisine is tailored to individual constitution and aims to bring harmony to the mind, body, and spirit.

Native American Corn-Based Diet: Many Native American tribes have a rich culinary tradition based on locally available ingredients. Corn, beans, and squash, known as the "Three Sisters," form the cornerstone of traditional diets. This combination provides a balanced array of nutrients and exemplifies the principles of sustainability and symbiosis.

Integrating Traditional Foods into Modern Lifestyles

Mindful Adaptation: In the context of modern lifestyles, the integration of traditional foods involves a mindful adaptation of culinary heritage. This adaptation may include selecting locally available ingredients, modifying recipes to align with dietary preferences, and incorporating traditional cooking methods into contemporary practices.

Culinary Exploration: Exploring traditional foods from various cultures opens the door to a diverse and enriching culinary experience. Trying new recipes, experimenting with different flavor profiles, and learning about the cultural context of dishes contribute to a broader understanding of global culinary heritage.

Community and Connection: Engaging in community-supported agriculture, farmers' markets, or local food initiatives provides an opportunity to connect with traditional foods sourced from the region. Supporting local producers fosters a sense of community and contributes to the sustainability of traditional agricultural practices.

Traditional Foods and Mindful Eating

Conscious Consumption: Mindful eating extends to the conscious consumption of traditional foods. Taking the time to savor each bite, appreciate the cultural significance of dishes, and engage in the sensory experience of eating enhances the grounding and nourishing qualities of traditional foods.

Gratitude for Culinary Heritage: Expressing gratitude for the culinary heritage embedded in traditional foods adds a dimension of mindfulness to meals. Recognizing the labor, knowledge, and cultural stories that contribute to each dish fosters a deeper appreciation for the nourishment provided.

Balancing Tradition and Individual Choices: In the pursuit of well-being, it's essential to balance the embrace of tradition with individual dietary preferences and health needs. Traditional foods can serve as a foundation, and modifications can be made to align with personal choices while preserving the essence of cultural heritage.

Culinary Wisdom for Grounding

Preserving Culinary Traditions: Preserving culinary traditions involves a collective effort to document, share, and pass down traditional recipes and cooking techniques. Families, communities, and cultural institutions play a role in safeguarding culinary heritage for future generations.

Education and Awareness: Raising awareness about the significance of traditional foods and the impact of culinary heritage on well-being is crucial. Educational initiatives, cooking classes, and community events contribute to a broader understanding of the value of traditional cuisines.

Sustainable Practices: Embracing traditional foods aligns with sustainable practices that promote biodiversity, support local agriculture, and reduce the environmental impact of food production. Traditional agricultural methods often prioritize ecological harmony and can inspire sustainable approaches to modern farming.

Conclusion: A Feast of Tradition and Well-Being

As we conclude our exploration of traditional foods for grounding, let the essence of culinary heritage linger—a celebration of flavors, stories, and the profound connection between food and well-being.

May the journey of embracing traditional foods be a feast—a banquet of cultural richness, ancestral wisdom, and the nourishing embrace of culinary heritage. As we transition to the subsequent chapters, may the spirit of traditional cuisines resonate—an invitation to savor the depth of tradition, embrace the wisdom of the past, and cultivate a grounded and well-nourished existence.

Mindful Cooking and Eating

In the bustling landscape of modern life, where time seems to slip through our fingers, the practice of mindful cooking and eating emerges as a beacon of presence and nourishment. This chapter invites us to explore the transformative power of slowing down, paying attention, and infusing intention into the acts of preparing and consuming food. From the rhythmic dance of chopping vegetables to the symphony of flavors on our taste buds, mindful cooking and eating provide a pathway to not only enhance the nutritional value of our meals but also to cultivate a deeper connection with the food we consume and the act of nourishing ourselves.

The Art of Mindful Cooking

Engaging the Senses: Mindful cooking begins with engaging the senses fully. As we approach the kitchen, we can appreciate the vibrant colors of fresh produce, inhale the aromatic dance of spices, feel the textures of ingredients, and listen to the sizzle and simmer of food being prepared. Engaging the senses not only brings us into the present moment but also enhances our connection to the culinary process.

Cultivating Presence: In the midst of our busy lives, the kitchen can be a sanctuary of presence. Mindful cooking involves being fully engaged in the task at hand, whether it's chopping vegetables, stirring a pot, or measuring ingredients. The rhythmic and repetitive nature of cooking can become a form of meditation, grounding us in the here and now.

Intentional Preparation: Mindful cooking invites us to infuse our preparations with intention. This goes beyond the mechanical act of following a recipe. It involves considering the nourishment each ingredient provides, the energy we bring to the cooking process, and the love and care we embed into the food we prepare. Cooking with intention transforms the kitchen into a sacred space of creation.

Mindful Eating Practices

Bringing Awareness to the Table: The practice of mindful eating extends beyond the kitchen and into the dining space. As we sit down to eat, we can bring awareness to the table. This involves setting an environment conducive to mindful eating—free from distractions, with a focus on the food before us. Creating a serene dining space contributes to a more intentional and pleasurable eating experience.

Savoring Each Bite: Mindful eating involves savoring each bite with full attention. Rather than rushing through a meal, we can take the time to appreciate the flavors, textures, and nuances of each bite. Savoring the eating experience enhances our enjoyment of food and fosters a deeper connection to the act of nourishing our bodies.

Chewing Mindfully: The simple act of chewing can become a gateway to mindfulness. Chewing each bite thoroughly not only aids digestion but also allows us to fully experience the taste and texture of our food. Mindful chewing is a practice in slowing down, promoting a sense of satiety, and fostering a mindful relationship with eating.

Mindful Cooking and Well-Being

Stress Reduction Through Cooking: Cooking, when approached mindfully, can be a therapeutic activity that reduces stress. The focus on the present moment, the tactile experience of handling ingredients, and the creative expression involved in cooking contribute to a sense of calm and relaxation. Cooking becomes a form of self-care that nourishes not only the body but also the mind.

Connection to Ingredients: Mindful cooking fosters a deeper connection to the ingredients we use. As we become more aware of the source, quality, and nutritional value of our ingredients, we develop a greater appreciation for the role each component plays in nourishing our bodies. This awareness can influence our choices, leading to a more balanced and healthful diet.

Culinary Creativity: Mindful cooking encourages culinary creativity and experimentation. By approaching cooking with a curious and open mindset, we can explore new recipes, flavors, and cooking techniques. The kitchen transforms into a canvas for creative expression, allowing us to infuse our meals with variety and excitement.

Mindful Cooking and Sustainability

Reducing Food Waste: Mindful cooking aligns with sustainability by promoting conscious consumption and reducing food waste. Planning meals mindfully, using ingredients efficiently, and repurposing leftovers contribute to a more sustainable approach to cooking. Mindful consideration of portion sizes also plays a role in minimizing food waste.

Supporting Local and Seasonal Eating: Mindful cooking involves a consideration of the environmental impact of our food choices. Supporting local and seasonal eating not only enhances the freshness and nutritional content of our meals but also contributes to sustainable agricultural practices. This approach aligns with the natural rhythms of the environment and supports local farmers.

Plant-Based and Flexitarian Choices: Mindful cooking can include a conscious consideration of the environmental footprint of our dietary choices. Choosing plant-based and flexitarian meals, which emphasize a predominance of plant foods and occasional inclusion of animal products, aligns with sustainability goals. These choices contribute to a more environmentally friendly and ethically conscious approach to eating.

Mindful Cooking as a Ritual

Culinary Rituals and Traditions: Mindful cooking can be infused with rituals and traditions that hold personal or cultural significance. Whether it's a morning tea ritual, a weekly family dinner tradition, or a special occasion meal preparation, these rituals add depth and meaning to the act of cooking. Rituals create a sense of continuity and connection to the past.

Mindful Meal Planning: Meal planning, when approached mindfully, becomes a strategic and intentional act. It involves considering nutritional needs, preferences, and the rhythm of daily life. Mindful meal planning supports a more organized approach to cooking, reducing the stress of last-minute decisions and ensuring a balance of flavors and nutrients in each meal.

Gratitude Practice: Infusing a gratitude practice into mindful cooking adds a layer of mindfulness to the culinary process. Expressing gratitude for the ingredients, the hands that prepared them, and the nourishment they provide cultivates a positive and appreciative mindset. Gratitude can be silently acknowledged or expressed through a mindful pause before eating.

Mindful Cooking and Cultural Connection

Preserving Culinary Heritage: For many, mindful cooking is a way to preserve and celebrate culinary heritage. Cooking traditional recipes passed down through generations becomes an act of cultural preservation. It involves not only the replication of flavors but also the transmission of stories, values, and a sense of identity embedded in each dish.

Culinary Exploration: Mindful cooking can also be a journey of culinary exploration, inviting individuals to try recipes from diverse cultures. Exploring global cuisines broadens culinary horizons, fosters an appreciation for cultural diversity, and adds a richness of flavors and techniques to one's repertoire.

Sharing the Table: The act of sharing a mindful meal becomes a profound form of cultural connection. Whether with family, friends, or neighbors, sharing a meal involves not only the exchange of food but also the sharing of stories, traditions, and a sense of belonging. The table becomes a space for cultural exchange and understanding.

Conclusion: The Alchemy of Mindful Cooking

As we conclude our exploration of mindful cooking and eating, let the alchemy of these practices linger—a reminder that the kitchen is not merely a place of culinary creation but a sanctuary for presence, connection, and nourishment.

May the journey of mindful cooking and eating be a celebration—an alchemical process that transforms daily meals into moments of mindfulness, gratitude, and well-being. As we transition to the subsequent chapters, may the spirit of mindful culinary practices resonate—an invitation to savor the richness of each ingredient, embrace the joy of cooking, and cultivate a mindful relationship with the nourishment that sustains us.

Nourishing Community

In the intricate tapestry of well-being, the thread of community intertwines with the choices we make about what we eat. The act of nourishing ourselves extends beyond the individual, reaching into the collective spaces we inhabit—our families, neighborhoods, and broader communities. This chapter explores the profound connection between healthy eating practices and community well-being. From communal gardens to shared meals, the choices we make about food have the power to strengthen the bonds that tie us together, foster a sense of belonging, and create a ripple effect of health and vitality.

The Collective Impact of Healthy Eating

Community as a Source of Support: Embarking on a journey of healthy eating is not a solitary endeavor. The support and encouragement of a community can be a powerful catalyst for sustained well-being. Whether it's sharing recipes, participating in group cooking classes, or engaging in collective wellness challenges, the community becomes a source of inspiration, motivation, and shared goals.

Culinary Knowledge Exchange: Within communities, there exists a wealth of culinary knowledge shaped by diverse cultural traditions and personal experiences. Healthy eating practices benefit from the exchange of this knowledge. Community members can share insights into traditional recipes, cooking techniques, and nutritional wisdom, creating a rich tapestry of culinary expertise.

Collective Accountability: Healthy eating becomes a shared commitment within a community, fostering a sense of collective accountability. When individuals come together with a common goal of well-being, there is a natural support system that encourages adherence to healthy choices. The shared journey creates an environment where the well-being of one member uplifts the entire community.

Community Gardens and Sustainable Eating

The Resurgence of Community Gardens: Community gardens have experienced a resurgence as hubs for sustainable and locally sourced produce. These shared green spaces provide community members with the opportunity to cultivate their own fruits and vegetables, fostering a direct connection to the food they consume. Community gardens promote sustainable agriculture, reduce food miles, and contribute to a sense of shared responsibility for the environment.

Teaching Sustainability Through Gardens: Community gardens offer a valuable platform for teaching sustainable eating practices. Beyond the act of planting and harvesting, these spaces provide opportunities for educational initiatives on composting, water conservation, and organic gardening methods. The lessons learned within community gardens extend to individual households, promoting sustainable practices in daily life.

Fostering Social Bonds: The act of tending to a community garden becomes a social activity that strengthens interpersonal bonds. Gardeners come together to share tips, celebrate harvests, and collaborate on the maintenance of the space. The shared experience of cultivating the land creates a sense of shared ownership and pride, contributing to the overall well-being of the community.

Shared Meals and Culinary Celebrations

The Significance of Shared Meals: Shared meals are a cornerstone of community life, transcending cultural and geographical boundaries. The act of gathering around a table to share food is a universal expression of connection, hospitality, and communal bonds. Shared meals foster a sense of belonging, provide an opportunity for social interaction, and contribute to the fabric of community life.

Potlucks and Culinary Diversity: Potluck gatherings exemplify the diversity and richness of community culinary traditions. Participants bring dishes reflective of their cultural backgrounds, family recipes, and personal preferences. These events become a celebration of culinary diversity, offering a tasting journey that transcends individual preferences and creates a tapestry of flavors.

Cooking Classes and Culinary Education: Community cooking classes serve as a platform for culinary education and skill-sharing. These classes provide practical knowledge about healthy cooking techniques, ingredient selection, and meal planning. By making culinary education accessible within communities, individuals are empowered to make informed choices that contribute to their well-being.

Food Accessibility and Equity

Addressing Food Deserts: Communities often face challenges related to food accessibility, with some areas designated as food deserts—places where access to fresh and nutritious food is limited. Addressing food deserts involves community-based initiatives such as mobile markets, community-supported agriculture (CSA) programs, and partnerships with local farmers. These efforts aim to bring fresh produce closer to residents, promoting health equity.

Community-Led Farmers' Markets: Farmers' markets led by the community provide a platform for local farmers and producers to connect directly with residents. These markets offer fresh, locally sourced produce and artisanal goods, fostering a sense of community pride and supporting regional agriculture. Community-led farmers' markets contribute to both economic vitality and healthful food options.

Collaborations with Local Producers: Communities can forge collaborations with local farmers and producers to establish a more direct and sustainable food supply chain. Initiatives such as community-supported agriculture (CSA) programs create partnerships between consumers and local farmers, ensuring a regular supply of fresh, seasonal produce to community members.

Building a Culture of Well-Being

Community Wellness Challenges: Community wellness challenges provide a structured and supportive framework for individuals to embark on health-focused journeys together. Whether it's a collective commitment to mindful eating, regular physical activity, or stress reduction practices, these challenges create a shared sense of purpose and encourage healthy habits.

Creating Health-Conscious Spaces: Communities can actively work to create environments that support health-conscious choices. This involves initiatives such as establishing walking trails, promoting outdoor activities, and incorporating green spaces into urban planning. Health-conscious spaces encourage physical activity, social interaction, and overall well-being.

Engaging Youth in Health Initiatives: Educating and engaging the youth within a community is pivotal for building a culture of well-being. School programs, community workshops, and extracurricular activities can instill the importance of healthy eating habits and an active lifestyle from an early age. Empowering the younger generation contributes to the sustainability of community well-being efforts.

Cultivating a Sense of Belonging

Social Connections Through Food: Food has a remarkable ability to create and strengthen social connections. Community gatherings centered around food—whether it's a neighborhood barbecue, a potluck dinner, or a community garden harvest festival—create opportunities for individuals to connect, share stories, and foster a sense of belonging.

Community Cookbook Initiatives: Creating community cookbooks becomes a collaborative endeavor that celebrates the culinary diversity within a community. Residents can contribute their favorite recipes, reflecting the cultural tapestry of the community. These cookbooks not only serve as culinary guides but also as tangible expressions of shared identity and unity.

Celebrating Cultural Festivals: Cultural festivals centered around food provide occasions for celebrating diversity, fostering understanding, and creating a sense of unity within a community. These events showcase the richness of culinary traditions, allowing residents to experience and appreciate the flavors of different cultures. Cultural festivals become expressions of inclusivity and mutual respect.

Conclusion: A Feast of Community Well-Being

As we conclude our exploration of nourishing community, let the essence of collective well-being linger—a reminder that the choices we make about food have the power to weave threads of connection, belonging, and vitality within the fabric of community life.

May the journey of nourishing community be a feast—a banquet of shared meals, collaborative gardens, and a tapestry of diverse culinary traditions. As we transition to the subsequent chapters, may the spirit of community well-being resonate—an invitation to savor the flavors of connection, cultivate a sense of belonging, and contribute to the thriving tapestry of communal health and vitality.

Chapter 6: Creative Expression
Finding Natural Talents

In the canvas of self-discovery and well-being, the exploration of creative expression unveils a transformative journey of self-realization. This chapter delves into the first stroke of this artistic exploration—finding and nurturing natural talents. From the rhythmic flow of brush on canvas to the melodic dance of fingers on piano keys, our natural talents are the brushes and instruments with which we paint the portrait of our inner selves. In this exploration, we navigate the landscapes of innate abilities, understanding the profound impact of creative expression on mental health, and unlocking the door to a more fulfilled and purposeful life.

Unveiling the Essence of Natural Talents

Defining Natural Talents: Natural talents are the inherent abilities, inclinations, and aptitudes that individuals possess from birth. These gifts, often unique to each person, can manifest in a variety of forms, including artistic expression, intellectual pursuits, physical abilities, and interpersonal skills. Recognizing and tapping into these innate talents is a key to unlocking a deeper understanding of oneself.

The Source of Joy and Flow: Natural talents are closely tied to activities that bring a sense of joy and flow. When engaged in activities that align with our innate abilities, time seems to lose its grip, and we enter a state of flow—a mental state where we are fully immersed and absorbed in the activity. This flow state not only brings intrinsic satisfaction but also serves as a pathway to enhanced well-being.

Nurturing Versus Acquiring: Distinguishing between natural talents and acquired skills is crucial. While acquired skills are developed through learning and practice, natural talents are intrinsic and often emerge effortlessly. Nurturing these innate abilities involves creating an environment that allows them to flourish, recognizing that the pursuit of one's natural talents can be a source of lifelong fulfillment.

The Multifaceted Nature of Natural Talents

Artistic Expression: For many, natural talents find expression in the arts—painting, drawing, sculpture, and various forms of visual expression. The act of creating art becomes a channel for self-expression, allowing individuals to communicate emotions, thoughts, and perspectives in a unique and personal way. Artistic talents encompass a wide spectrum, from fine arts to digital media, each offering a distinct avenue for creative exploration.

Musical Aptitude: Natural talents often reveal themselves through a deep connection to music. Musical aptitude extends beyond playing instruments or singing; it includes an innate sense of rhythm, melody, and harmony. Engaging with music becomes a profound means of self-expression, emotional release, and a source of joy. Musical talents can manifest in various forms, from playing instruments to composing original pieces.

Physical Prowess: Physical talents encompass a range of abilities, from sports to dance and movement arts. Some individuals naturally excel in physical activities, finding joy and fulfillment in the coordination of body and mind.

Whether it's the grace of a dancer, the precision of an athlete, or the fluidity of a martial artist, physical talents provide avenues for self-discovery and well-being.

Intellectual Gifts: Natural talents are not limited to the realm of the arts or physical abilities; they also manifest in intellectual pursuits. Some individuals possess a natural affinity for problem-solving, critical thinking, or creative ideation. Intellectual talents can be expressed through writing, scientific inquiry, mathematical endeavors, or innovative thinking, contributing to personal and societal advancement.

Discovering Your Unique Gifts

Self-Reflection and Exploration: The journey of discovering natural talents begins with self-reflection and exploration. Taking time to reflect on activities that bring joy, moments of flow, and a sense of fulfillment provides insight into innate abilities. Experimenting with a variety of activities, whether artistic, intellectual, or physical, allows individuals to uncover hidden talents and passions.

Feedback from Others: The perspectives of others can offer valuable insights into our natural talents. Friends, family, and mentors may observe strengths and aptitudes that we might overlook. Seeking feedback and engaging in open conversations about personal strengths can illuminate aspects of our natural talents that may not be immediately apparent.

Personality Assessments: Personality assessments, such as the Myers-Briggs Type Indicator (MBTI), StrengthsFinder, or the Enneagram, can provide structured frameworks for understanding personal strengths and preferences. These assessments offer insights into areas where individuals naturally excel, guiding them toward activities that align with their unique gifts.

The Impact of Natural Talents on Mental Health

Enhancing Self-Esteem: Embracing and utilizing natural talents positively influences self-esteem. Engaging in activities that align with innate abilities fosters a sense of mastery and accomplishment. The positive feedback loop created by the pursuit of natural talents contributes to a healthy self-image and a greater sense of self-worth.

Stress Reduction and Relaxation: Creative expression through natural talents serves as a powerful tool for stress reduction and relaxation. The immersive nature of activities that align with innate abilities—whether it's painting, playing an instrument, or engaging in a physical activity—creates a meditative space that promotes mental well-being. The release of stress through creative expression contributes to overall emotional balance.

Fostering Emotional Resilience: Natural talents provide an outlet for emotional expression and resilience. When faced with challenges, individuals often turn to their creative pursuits to navigate and process emotions. Whether it's writing as a form of catharsis, creating visual art to express complex feelings, or playing music to evoke specific emotions, natural talents become a refuge for emotional resilience.

Nurturing Natural Talents in Daily Life

Incorporating Creativity into Routine: Nurturing natural talents involves integrating creative expression into daily life. This can be as simple as incorporating short creative breaks into a work routine, dedicating time to artistic endeavors, or infusing creative elements into everyday tasks. Making space for creative expression becomes a commitment to personal well-being.

Creating a Dedicated Workspace: Establishing a dedicated workspace for creative pursuits enhances the nurturing of natural talents. Whether it's a corner for painting, a music studio, or a writing nook, having a designated space fosters a conducive environment for creative expression. This space serves as a sanctuary for exploration and self-discovery.

Setting Realistic Goals: Setting realistic and achievable goals is essential in nurturing natural talents. Goals provide a sense of direction and purpose, guiding individuals in their creative pursuits. Breaking down larger objectives into smaller, manageable tasks ensures a steady and fulfilling progression on the journey of self-expression.

Collaborative Creativity and Community Connection

Collaborative Projects: Natural talents can find new dimensions in collaborative projects. Engaging in creative collaborations with others—whether it's joining a band, participating in community art projects, or contributing to group initiatives—creates a dynamic exchange of ideas and fosters a sense of community. Collaborative creativity amplifies the impact of individual talents.

Community Arts Programs: Participating in community arts programs provides a platform for showcasing and further developing natural talents. Local art exhibitions, musical performances, and community theater productions offer opportunities for individuals to connect with like-minded creatives, share their talents with the community, and contribute to the cultural richness of the locality.

Mentorship and Learning Communities: Engaging in mentorship relationships or joining learning communities supports the growth of natural talents. Learning from experienced individuals in the field, receiving constructive feedback, and sharing experiences with peers create a nurturing environment for continuous learning and development.

Conclusion: The Symphony of Self-Expression

As we conclude our exploration of finding natural talents, let the symphony of self-expression linger—a reminder that within each of us lies a unique melody waiting to be heard. The journey of discovering and nurturing natural talents is not just a pursuit of creative expression; it is a pathway to self-discovery, well-being, and a life infused with purpose.

May the exploration of natural talents be a symphony—a harmonious blend of creativity, joy, and the unveiling of one's authentic self. As we transition to the subsequent chapters, may the spirit of creative expression resonate—an invitation to explore the vast landscape of innate abilities, paint the canvas of our inner worlds, and dance to the rhythm of our unique gifts.

Learning New Skills

In the tapestry of self-discovery and well-being, the thread of continuous learning weaves a narrative of growth and transformation. This chapter embarks on the exploration of acquiring new skills—an endeavor that goes hand in hand with creative expression. Learning new skills is not only a journey of acquiring practical abilities but also a profound exploration of personal potential and an avenue for expanding the palette of creative expression. From the strokes of a brush to the chords of a musical instrument, the act of learning new skills is a dynamic and enriching process that fosters resilience, enhances cognitive function, and opens doors to uncharted territories of self-discovery.

The Dynamics of Lifelong Learning

Embracing a Growth Mindset: At the heart of learning new skills is the cultivation of a growth mindset. Embracing a growth mindset means viewing challenges and obstacles as opportunities for growth rather than insurmountable barriers. Individuals with a growth mindset approach learning with enthusiasm, resilience, and a belief in their capacity to acquire new skills through dedication and effort.

The Intersection of Curiosity and Learning: Curiosity is the driving force behind lifelong learning. The desire to explore, understand, and engage with the world fuels the process of acquiring new skills. Cultivating curiosity involves asking questions, seeking novel experiences, and maintaining an open-minded approach to learning. Curiosity transforms the acquisition of skills into a dynamic and ever-evolving journey.

Learning as a Form of Self-Expression: Learning new skills is an act of self-expression—an avenue through which individuals communicate their evolving identities and aspirations. Whether it's learning to play a musical instrument, mastering a new language, or acquiring a creative craft, each skill acquired becomes a brushstroke on the canvas of personal expression. Learning is a testament to the inherent human drive for growth and self-discovery.

The Cognitive Benefits of Learning

Neuroplasticity and Cognitive Flexibility: Engaging in the process of learning stimulates neuroplasticity—the brain's ability to reorganize and form new neural connections. Learning new skills enhances cognitive flexibility, enabling individuals to adapt to new information, think creatively, and approach challenges with a versatile mindset. The cognitive benefits of learning extend beyond the specific skill acquired, influencing overall brain health.

Memory Enhancement: Learning new skills challenges the memory systems of the brain, contributing to memory enhancement. Whether memorizing musical notes, language vocabulary, or procedural steps in a new skill, the brain undergoes adaptive changes that strengthen memory retention. These improvements in memory function extend to other areas of cognitive performance, fostering an overall cognitive vitality.

Cognitive Reserve and Aging: The concept of cognitive reserve suggests that engaging in intellectually stimulating activities, such as learning new skills, builds a reserve of cognitive resources that may offset the effects of aging and age-related cognitive decline. Lifelong learning becomes a proactive approach to maintaining cognitive health and resilience throughout the lifespan.

The Resilience of the Learning Mindset

Embracing Challenges and Failures: Learning new skills inevitably involves challenges and, at times, failures. Embracing challenges and reframing failures as opportunities for growth fosters resilience. Individuals with a learning mindset view setbacks not as indicators of inability but as stepping stones on the path to mastery. This resilience contributes to a positive and adaptive approach to life's challenges.

Perseverance and Grit: The journey of acquiring new skills requires perseverance and grit. Perseverance involves the ability to persist in the face of challenges, setbacks, and moments of frustration. Grit, a concept introduced by psychologist Angela Duckworth, encompasses passion and sustained effort toward long-term goals. Cultivating perseverance and grit through learning new skills strengthens the capacity for resilience in various aspects of life.

Adaptability in a Changing World: In a rapidly evolving world, adaptability is a valuable trait. Learning new skills nurtures adaptability by fostering a mindset of continuous growth and flexibility. The ability to acquire and apply new knowledge and skills positions individuals to navigate change, seize opportunities, and thrive in dynamic environments.

The Transformative Power of Learning

Personal Empowerment: Learning new skills empowers individuals to take an active role in shaping their lives. Whether acquiring practical skills for daily tasks or delving into creative pursuits, the process of learning fosters a sense of autonomy and personal agency. This empowerment extends beyond the specific skill acquired, influencing individuals' perceptions of their own capabilities.

Expanding Horizons: Learning new skills opens doors to unexplored territories and expands horizons. Whether learning a new language to connect with different cultures, acquiring a technical skill to navigate a digital landscape, or delving into the arts to unlock creative expression, each new skill acquired broadens the spectrum of possibilities and enriches life experiences.

Cultivating a Growth-Oriented Identity: The act of learning becomes an integral part of one's identity. Cultivating a growth-oriented identity involves seeing oneself as a perpetual learner, capable of evolving, adapting, and acquiring new skills throughout life. This identity shift influences the way individuals approach challenges, view setbacks, and perceive their own potential.

Strategies for Effective Learning

Setting Clear Goals: Effective learning begins with setting clear and achievable goals. Whether the goal is to learn a new language, master a musical instrument, or acquire a technical skill, articulating specific objectives provides a roadmap for the learning journey. Clear goals create a sense of direction and purpose.

Creating a Structured Learning Plan: Developing a structured learning plan involves breaking down larger goals into smaller, manageable tasks. A structured plan includes a timeline, milestones, and a sequence of steps to guide the learning process. Having a well-defined plan fosters a sense of organization and ensures steady progress.

Balancing Challenge and Skill: The concept of "flow," introduced by psychologist Mihaly Csikszentmihalyi, emphasizes the importance of balancing challenge and skill in the learning process. Activities that match an individual's skill level with the level of challenge create an optimal state of engagement and flow. Balancing challenge and skill sustains motivation and enhances the overall learning experience.

Learning New Skills for Creative Expression

Creative Skills as a Form of Self-Expression: Learning creative skills, whether in the arts, music, or other expressive domains, becomes a powerful channel for self-expression. Creative skills enable individuals to communicate emotions, ideas, and perspectives in unique and personalized ways. Engaging in the process of learning creative skills transforms the act of expression into a dynamic and evolving journey.

Interdisciplinary Learning: Creativity often flourishes at the intersections of different disciplines. Embracing interdisciplinary learning involves exploring connections between seemingly unrelated areas. For example, combining music and visual arts or integrating technology with traditional crafts can lead to innovative and unique forms of creative expression. Interdisciplinary learning broadens the creative landscape.

Exploring Diverse Learning Modalities: Individuals have diverse learning preferences and modalities. Some may thrive in hands-on, experiential learning, while others prefer visual or auditory learning. Exploring diverse learning modalities, such as workshops, online courses, mentorship programs, or collaborative learning environments, allows individuals to discover the approaches that resonate most effectively with their learning styles.

The Role of Mentorship in Learning

Guidance and Support: Mentorship plays a pivotal role in the learning journey. Having a mentor provides guidance, support, and insights based on the mentor's own experiences. Mentors offer valuable perspectives, share practical knowledge, and contribute to the mentee's growth and development. Mentorship fosters a sense of community and shared learning.

Building a Learning Community: Learning is often more enriching when it occurs within a community. Building a learning community involves connecting with peers who share similar interests and goals. Learning communities provide opportunities for collaboration, idea exchange, and mutual support. Online forums, local meetups, and collaborative projects contribute to the communal aspect of learning.

Reciprocal Learning: Mentorship is not a one-way street; it involves reciprocal learning. Mentors benefit from the exchange of ideas, fresh perspectives, and the opportunity to refine their own skills through teaching. Reciprocal learning creates a dynamic and mutually supportive relationship, where both mentor and mentee contribute to each other's growth.

Conclusion: A Symphony of Continuous Growth

As we conclude our exploration of learning new skills, let the symphony of continuous growth linger—a reminder that the journey of acquiring new abilities is not just a path to practical proficiency but a dynamic process of self-discovery and personal evolution.

May the exploration of learning new skills be a symphony—a harmonious blend of curiosity, resilience, and the unveiling of untapped potentials. As we transition to the subsequent chapters, may the spirit of continuous learning resonate—an invitation to embrace challenges, cultivate a growth-oriented mindset, and dance to the rhythm of lifelong discovery.

Sharing Your Light

In the realm of creative expression, the act of sharing one's light illuminates the transformative power of artistic endeavors. This chapter delves into the profound significance of sharing creative work with the world. From the strokes of a paintbrush to the words penned in a novel, the creative process extends its radiance when shared. The journey of sharing one's light is a dynamic interplay between vulnerability, connection, and the potential to inspire and uplift others. As we explore this theme, we uncover the layers of intention, impact, and the communal spirit that weaves through the fabric of creative expression.

The Essence of Sharing Creative Work

A Manifestation of Vulnerability: Sharing creative work is an act of vulnerability—an offering of one's innermost thoughts, emotions, and artistic creations to the scrutiny of others. It involves opening the door to the private chambers of the soul and allowing others to witness the intricacies of personal expression. In this vulnerability, there lies a profound authenticity that resonates with the human experience.

Connecting Through Shared Stories: At its core, creative expression is a shared storytelling experience. Whether through visual arts, literature, music, or any other form, creative works tell stories that transcend individual narratives. Sharing these stories creates connections— threads of understanding that weave through diverse lives, fostering empathy, and forming bridges between different perspectives.

Inspiring and Uplifting Others: The act of sharing creative work has the power to inspire and uplift others. Whether through the evocative brushstrokes of a painting, the emotional cadence of a song, or the vivid imagery of a poem, creative works have the ability to touch hearts, provoke thought, and spark inspiration. The shared light of creativity becomes a beacon that guides others on their own journeys.

Intention and Authentic Expression

Clarifying Intentions: Before sharing creative work, clarifying intentions becomes a foundational step. Understanding the purpose behind sharing—whether it's to evoke emotions, convey a message, or simply to connect with others—provides a roadmap for the creative journey. Intentions shape the way creative work is presented, influencing the impact it has on both the creator and the audience.

Balancing Authenticity and Audience Consideration: Navigating the balance between authenticity and consideration for the audience is an art in itself. While authenticity infuses creative work with genuine emotion and depth, considering the audience ensures that the message is communicated effectively. Striking this balance involves staying true to one's voice while being mindful of the diverse perspectives of potential viewers, readers, or listeners.

Transparency in Process: Sharing not only the final product but also the creative process itself adds an extra layer of authenticity. Whether through behind-the-scenes glimpses, artist statements, or personal reflections, transparency in the creative process invites the audience into the creator's world. It fosters a sense of connection and understanding, allowing others to witness the evolution of an idea into its final form.

Overcoming the Fear of Judgment

Embracing the Vulnerability of Exposure: The fear of judgment is a common hurdle when it comes to sharing creative work. Embracing the vulnerability of exposure involves acknowledging this fear and understanding that it is a natural part of the creative process. It requires recognizing that the act of sharing is an invitation for connection rather than a plea for validation.

Shifting Focus from Approval to Connection: Shifting the focus from seeking approval to fostering connection transforms the narrative around sharing creative work. Instead of measuring success solely through external validation, the emphasis turns toward the impact on the audience and the connections forged through shared experiences. This shift liberates creators from the constraints of external judgment.

Cultivating Resilience in Creativity: Cultivating resilience in the face of potential criticism or judgment is a key aspect of sharing one's light. Resilience involves understanding that creative work is inherently subjective and that not every response will be positive. It means learning from feedback, discerning constructive criticism from personal attacks, and using challenges as opportunities for growth.

Platforms for Sharing Creative Work

Online Platforms and Social Media: The digital era has brought forth a plethora of online platforms and social media channels that provide creators with unprecedented opportunities to share their work. From visual platforms like Instagram and Pinterest to literary platforms like Medium, these spaces enable creators to reach global audiences, connect with like-minded individuals, and receive real-time feedback.

Creative Communities and Collaborations: Joining creative communities and engaging in collaborations enhances the sharing experience. Creative communities, whether local or online, offer spaces for mutual support, feedback, and shared inspiration. Collaborative projects bring together diverse talents, fostering a sense of collective creation and amplifying the impact of individual contributions.

Public Performances and Exhibitions: Public performances, exhibitions, and live events provide tangible avenues for sharing creative work. Whether it's performing music on stage, showcasing visual art in a gallery, or reading poetry at an open mic, these experiences allow creators to directly connect with an audience, receive immediate reactions, and witness the impact of their work in a physical space.

The Impact of Shared Light

Creating Ripples of Inspiration: The impact of shared light extends beyond the immediate audience. Creative works, when shared, have the potential to create ripples of inspiration that reach unexpected shores. The resonance of a powerful painting, a moving piece of music, or a compelling story can inspire others to embark on their creative journeys, creating a ripple effect of artistic exploration.

Fostering Empathy and Understanding: Creative expression is a universal language that transcends cultural, linguistic, and geographic boundaries. When shared, creative works foster empathy and understanding by providing glimpses into different perspectives, experiences, and emotions. The shared light of creativity becomes a bridge that connects diverse individuals through the shared human experience.

Building Community and Shared Identity: The act of sharing creative work contributes to the building of communities and shared identities. Whether within niche artistic circles or broader cultural movements, shared creative experiences create a sense of belonging. Communities formed around shared artistic interests become spaces for mutual support, collaboration, and the celebration of diverse expressions.

Navigating Critique and Feedback

Discerning Constructive Criticism: Receiving critique is an inherent part of sharing creative work. Discerning constructive criticism involves separating feedback that contributes to growth from unfounded negativity. Constructive criticism provides insights, suggestions, and perspectives that can enhance the creative process, refine skills, and elevate the quality of future work.

Celebrating Positive Feedback: Celebrating positive feedback is a vital aspect of the creative journey. Acknowledging and appreciating the impact of one's work on others reinforces the sense of purpose and fulfillment that comes from creative expression. Positive feedback serves as encouragement, validating the creator's efforts and inspiring continued exploration.

Continuous Growth Through Feedback: Embracing a mindset of continuous growth through feedback transforms the creative process into an evolving journey. Whether the feedback is positive or critical, viewing it as an opportunity for improvement, refinement, and expansion cultivates a dynamic and resilient approach to creativity. Each piece of feedback becomes a stepping stone on the path of artistic development.

Conclusion: Illuminating the World with Creativity

As we conclude our exploration of sharing your light, let the glow of creative expression linger—a reminder that the act of sharing goes beyond self-expression to become a beacon of inspiration and connection.

May the exploration of sharing creative work be an illumination—a radiant interplay of vulnerability, intention, and the weaving of shared stories. As we transition to the subsequent chapters, may the spirit of shared light resonate—an invitation to embrace the transformative power of creativity, connect with others through shared expression, and continue to illuminate the world with the unique brilliance of artistic endeavors.

Receiving Others' Gifts

In the symphony of creative expression, the melody of reciprocity emerges when we open our hearts to receive the gifts of others. This chapter explores the art of receiving—acknowledging and appreciating the creative works of fellow artists, writers, musicians, and creators. The act of receiving others' gifts is a dance of connection, a shared celebration of diverse expressions, and a pathway to inspiration and mutual growth. As we explore this theme, we uncover the nuances of openness, gratitude, and the transformative impact of embracing the artistic contributions of others.

The Beauty of Openness

Cultivating an Open Mind: Receiving others' gifts begins with cultivating an open mind—a willingness to explore, appreciate, and engage with a diverse array of creative expressions. An open mind embraces the richness of different perspectives, styles, and genres. It allows for the discovery of unexpected treasures and the expansion of one's own artistic horizons.

Breaking Down Barriers: Openness involves breaking down barriers that may hinder the reception of others' gifts. Preconceived notions, biases, and rigid expectations can create walls that block the flow of creative energy. Breaking down these barriers invites a free exchange of ideas, fosters a sense of inclusivity, and allows for the emergence of new and inspiring artistic influences.

Exploring Unfamiliar Territories: Receiving others' gifts often involves venturing into unfamiliar territories. Exploring creative works outside one's comfort zone exposes individuals to new genres, styles, and cultural influences.

Stepping into the unknown provides opportunities for personal growth, the discovery of hidden gems, and the cultivation of a more nuanced appreciation for the vast spectrum of creative expression.

Gratitude and Recognition

The Power of Gratitude: Gratitude forms the heart of receiving others' gifts. Expressing gratitude for the creative contributions of fellow artists acknowledges the time, effort, and emotional investment that goes into artistic endeavors. Gratitude creates a positive energy loop, nurturing a culture of appreciation within creative communities and fostering a sense of interconnectedness.

Recognizing the Shared Journey: In receiving others' gifts, it's essential to recognize the shared journey of the creative process. Every artistic creation is a culmination of experiences, inspirations, and the artist's unique voice. Acknowledging the shared aspects of the creative journey builds a sense of camaraderie and reinforces the understanding that each contribution adds to the collective tapestry of human expression.

Honoring Diverse Perspectives: Receiving others' gifts involves honoring diverse perspectives and recognizing the value of different voices. Creative expressions are deeply influenced by individual experiences, cultural backgrounds, and personal narratives. Honoring this diversity contributes to the richness of creative conversations, fosters cross-cultural understanding, and promotes a more inclusive artistic landscape.

Embracing Inspiration and Influence

The Flow of Creative Energy: Receiving others' gifts creates a dynamic flow of creative energy. Inspiration often arises from the interplay of different artistic voices, styles, and themes. Embracing the flow of creative energy involves allowing oneself to be inspired by the work of others—finding resonance, connecting with emotions, and letting the echoes of others' creativity contribute to the evolution of one's own artistic voice.

Navigating Influence and Originality: The relationship between influence and originality is a delicate dance in the creative realm. Receiving others' gifts may influence one's own creative expression, and this influence can be a source of growth and inspiration. Navigating this dynamic involves balancing the appreciation of influence with the commitment to authenticity, ensuring that personal expression remains true to one's unique voice.

Evolution Through Cross-Pollination: Cross-pollination of ideas and styles occurs when creators actively engage in receiving and responding to the gifts of others. This exchange fosters an environment of continuous evolution and innovation. The blending of different artistic elements leads to the emergence of new genres, movements, and forms of expression, demonstrating the transformative power of shared creativity.

Constructive Engagement with Others' Work

Active Listening and Observation: Receiving others' gifts requires active listening and observation. Whether it's listening to music, observing visual art, or reading literature, engaging with the work of others involves a receptive state of mind. Active listening goes beyond surface appreciation, delving into the nuances of composition, structure, and the artist's intent.

Reflective Engagement: Reflective engagement with others' work involves taking the time to contemplate and internalize the impact of creative expressions. It may include personal reflections, journaling, or discussions with fellow enthusiasts. Reflective engagement deepens the connection with the work, allowing for a more profound understanding of the artist's message and the emotional resonance of the piece.

Contribution to Constructive Dialogue: Receiving others' gifts becomes a meaningful part of a larger creative dialogue. Constructive engagement involves contributing to discussions, sharing insights, and providing thoughtful feedback. This dialogue extends beyond mere appreciation, creating a space for meaningful conversations that contribute to the growth and development of artistic communities.

Nurturing a Supportive Creative Ecosystem

Celebrating Diversity in Creativity: Nurturing a supportive creative ecosystem involves celebrating the diversity of creative expressions. Recognizing and celebrating different styles, themes, and forms of artistic communication contributes to a vibrant and inclusive artistic community. Celebrating diversity creates a space where creators feel empowered to explore their unique voices without fear of judgment.

Supporting Emerging Artists: Receiving others' gifts includes actively supporting emerging artists on their creative journeys. This support can take various forms, such as attending exhibitions, purchasing artwork, sharing works on social media, or offering mentorship. Supporting emerging artists contributes to the sustainability of the creative ecosystem and encourages a new generation of voices to flourish.

Collaborative Opportunities: A supportive creative ecosystem fosters collaborative opportunities. Whether through joint exhibitions, interdisciplinary projects, or collective initiatives, collaboration enhances the interconnectedness of creative communities. Collaborative projects provide platforms for cross-pollination of ideas, shared learning, and the creation of collective works that transcend individual contributions.

Overcoming Comparison and Cultivating Appreciation

Overcoming the Comparison Trap: Receiving others' gifts can sometimes trigger the comparison trap, where individuals may feel inadequate or envious of others' talents. Overcoming this trap involves recognizing that each creative journey is unique and that everyone is on their path of growth. Cultivating self-compassion and focusing on personal development helps overcome the detrimental effects of comparison.

Cultivating Appreciation Without Judgment: Cultivating appreciation without judgment is a key aspect of receiving others' gifts. It involves appreciating the unique qualities of each creative work without imposing subjective value judgments. Recognizing that artistic expressions are diverse and subjective allows for a more open-hearted and non-judgmental reception of others' contributions.

Transformative Power of Genuine Appreciation: Genuine appreciation has a transformative power that extends beyond the immediate moment. When individuals authentically appreciate others' gifts, it creates a positive ripple effect within the creative ecosystem. Genuine appreciation builds a culture of encouragement, kindness, and mutual support, fostering an environment where every artist feels seen, valued, and motivated to continue their creative exploration.

Conclusion: A Tapestry Woven with Shared Gifts

As we conclude our exploration of receiving others' gifts, let the threads of connection and appreciation linger—a reminder that the act of receiving is not only about acknowledging the talents of others but also about weaving a tapestry of shared creativity.

May the exploration of receiving others' gifts be a tapestry—a vibrant interplay of openness, gratitude, and the celebration of diverse expressions. As we transition to the subsequent chapters, may the spirit of shared gifts resonate—an invitation to embrace the beauty of interconnected creativity, support fellow artists on their journeys, and continue to contribute to the rich tapestry of the creative world.

Chapter 7: Touchstones for Reminding Yourself of Purpose
Totems From Nature

In the symphony of self-discovery and purpose, nature stands as a timeless muse and teacher. This chapter explores the concept of totems from nature—symbols, elements, and patterns found in the natural world that serve as touchstones, grounding individuals in their purpose and reminding them of the interconnectedness of life. As we delve into this theme, we embark on a journey through the landscapes of mindfulness, symbolism, and the profound wisdom that nature offers as a guide for living with purpose.

The Language of Nature

Nature as a Reflective Mirror: Nature has a remarkable ability to reflect aspects of the human experience. From the cycles of growth and decay to the intricate balance of ecosystems, nature serves as a reflective mirror for the patterns and rhythms inherent in life. Totems from nature, therefore, become mirrors that allow individuals to contemplate their own journeys and align with the universal flow of existence.

Symbolism in the Natural World: Symbols drawn from nature carry rich layers of meaning that resonate across cultures and generations. A tree, for example, symbolizes strength, growth, and interconnectedness. Water signifies fluidity, adaptability, and the flow of life. Animals often embody specific qualities—wisdom, resilience, or grace. Exploring the symbolism embedded in the natural world unveils a language that speaks to the core of human aspirations and purpose.

Connecting with the Elemental Forces: The elements—earth, water, air, fire—form the building blocks of the natural world. Each element holds unique qualities and energies that can be harnessed as sources of inspiration and guidance. Connecting with the elemental forces involves recognizing the parallels between these fundamental aspects of nature and the elemental qualities within oneself. Totems from nature become conduits for tapping into the elemental wisdom that resides both in the external world and the internal landscape.

Totems From Nature: A Path to Mindful Living

Trees as Symbols of Resilience: Trees stand as ancient sentinels, witnessing the passage of time and seasons. Their roots delve deep into the earth, providing stability, while their branches reach for the sky, symbolizing growth and expansion. Totems from trees inspire individuals to cultivate resilience, grounding themselves in their roots while reaching for the heights of their aspirations. The annual cycle of shedding leaves and welcoming new growth mirrors the process of letting go and embracing transformation.

Water as a Metaphor for Adaptability: Water, with its fluid and adaptive nature, serves as a powerful metaphor for the ebb and flow of life. Totems from water encourage individuals to embrace change with grace, recognizing that, like a river finding its course, life's journey may take unexpected turns. The ability to adapt, shift, and navigate challenges becomes a guiding principle for living with purpose.

Animals as Messengers of Wisdom: Animals, with their diverse characteristics and behaviors, often carry symbolic significance in various cultures. Totems from animals serve as messengers of wisdom, offering insights into different aspects of life. For example, the owl, often associated with wisdom, encourages reflective contemplation. The salmon, known for its perseverance in swimming upstream, symbolizes determination in the face of obstacles. Exploring the symbolism of animals becomes a journey of uncovering valuable lessons and qualities to integrate into one's purposeful living.

Communing with the Seasons

Spring: The Season of Renewal: Spring, with its blossoming flowers and rejuvenated landscapes, symbolizes renewal and new beginnings. Totems from the spring season inspire individuals to embrace the energy of fresh starts, growth, and the blooming of creative potential. The emergence of life after the dormancy of winter becomes a touchstone for reconnecting with the vitality of purpose.

Summer: Abundance and Fulfillment: Summer, characterized by abundance and warmth, represents a season of fulfillment. Totems from the summer months encourage individuals to bask in the fruits of their labor, recognizing achievements, and celebrating milestones. The abundance of nature during this season becomes a reminder of the richness that purposeful living can bring.

Autumn: Embracing Change and Harvest: Autumn, with its falling leaves and the harvest season, symbolizes change and the fruition of efforts. Totems from autumn guide individuals to gracefully navigate transitions, recognizing that letting go is an integral part of the cycle of life. The act of harvesting, reaping what has been sown, becomes a metaphor for the rewards that come with purposeful endeavors.

Winter: Reflection and Inner Growth: Winter, a season of dormancy and quiet reflection, invites individuals to turn inward. Totems from winter encourage a contemplative exploration of inner landscapes, fostering personal growth during moments of stillness. The stark beauty of winter landscapes becomes a touchstone for the transformative power of introspection and the preparation for new cycles of growth.

Nature's Timeless Rituals

Sunrise and Sunset: Markers of Beginnings and Endings: The daily rhythm of sunrise and sunset serves as a natural ritual, marking the beginning and ending of each day. Totems from these celestial events inspire individuals to embrace the cyclical nature of life, finding purpose in each new dawn and reflecting on the experiences of the day as the sun sets. The ritual of sunrise and sunset becomes a daily reminder of the continuity and preciousness of time.

Moon Phases: Navigating Cycles and Change: The changing phases of the moon symbolize cycles, rhythms, and the inevitability of change. Totems from the moon's journey encourage individuals to navigate life's cycles with an understanding that change is both constant and transformative. The waxing and waning of the moon become metaphors for the cyclical nature of personal growth and the rhythmic dance of purpose.

Changing Seasons: Embracing the Fluidity of Life: The changing seasons, from spring to winter and back again, represent the fluidity of life's journey. Totems from nature's seasonal transitions guide individuals to embrace the inherent changes in their own lives, recognizing that each season contributes to the richness of the whole. The cyclical nature of seasons becomes a touchstone for navigating the inevitable changes and transformations on the path of purpose.

Rituals for Connecting with Totems From Nature

Nature Walks and Mindful Observation: Engaging in nature walks and mindful observation provides opportunities to connect with totems from nature. Paying attention to the details of the natural world—textures, colors, sounds—facilitates a deeper connection with the symbolic elements present. Nature walks become rituals for tuning into the wisdom that the environment offers as a source of guidance and inspiration.

Creating Nature Altars: Creating nature altars, whether in indoor spaces or outdoor sanctuaries, becomes a ritual for bringing totems from nature into daily life. Collecting symbolic elements such as stones, leaves, feathers, or other treasures during walks and arranging them with intention creates a tangible and sacred space for reflection and connection.

Seasonal Celebrations and Reflections: Honoring the changing seasons through seasonal celebrations and reflections becomes a ritual for aligning with the rhythms of nature. Setting aside moments for contemplation, journaling, or creative expression during significant seasonal transitions provides opportunities for individuals to connect with the symbolic meanings of each season and integrate those insights into their purposeful living.

Nature's Wisdom as a Guide

Silent Contemplation in Natural Settings: Engaging in silent contemplation in natural settings becomes a practice for attuning oneself to the wisdom of totems from nature. Whether by a serene lake, in a forest, or atop a mountain, moments of stillness in natural environments allow individuals to listen to the subtle whispers of the earth. Silent contemplation becomes a touchstone for receiving guidance and clarity on their purposeful journey.

Meditation with Natural Imagery: Incorporating natural imagery into meditation practices becomes a powerful ritual for connecting with totems from nature on a deeper level. Visualizing elements such as trees, water, animals, or celestial bodies during meditation sessions creates an inner sanctuary where individuals can draw strength, insight, and inspiration from the symbolic language of nature.

Symbolic Integration into Daily Life: Integrating totems from nature into daily life becomes an ongoing ritual for staying connected with purpose. Whether through wearing symbolic jewelry, incorporating natural elements into home decor, or setting nature-inspired intentions, individuals carry the wisdom of totems with them as reminders of their guiding principles. This integration becomes a seamless thread woven into the fabric of daily existence.

Conclusion: Totems From Nature as Guides on the Journey

As we conclude our exploration of totems from nature, let the echoes of natural wisdom linger—a reminder that the beauty of purposeful living is intricately woven into the landscapes of the earth.

May the exploration of totems from nature be a guide—a mindful interplay of symbolism, connection, and the perennial wisdom that nature generously imparts. As we transition to the subsequent chapters, may the spirit of totems from nature resonate—an invitation to ground oneself in purpose, find inspiration in the world around, and continue to tread the path with the guidance of nature's timeless symbols.

Inspirational Quotes

In the mosaic of purposeful living, words have the power to act as beacons of inspiration, guiding individuals on their journey. This chapter delves into the world of inspirational quotes—wisdom distilled into succinct phrases that serve as touchstones, offering guidance, motivation, and reminders of the deeper meaning behind one's pursuits. As we explore this theme, we unravel the art of language as a tool for self-discovery, resilience, and the continuous realignment with purpose.

The Essence of Inspirational Quotes

The Alchemy of Words: Inspirational quotes possess a unique alchemy—they distill complex emotions, experiences, and wisdom into a few carefully chosen words. This alchemy transforms language into a potent elixir that resonates with individuals, stirring a profound response within. The essence of inspirational quotes lies in their ability to encapsulate universal truths, offering timeless insights that transcend the boundaries of time and culture.

Language as a Catalyst for Change: Language, when wielded with intention, becomes a catalyst for personal and societal transformation. Inspirational quotes act as linguistic catalysts, igniting the flames of positive change within individuals. The resonance of carefully crafted words has the power to shift perspectives, elevate moods, and propel individuals into action, setting the stage for meaningful transformation on the path to purpose.

Connection Through Shared Language: Inspirational quotes create a language of connection—a shared vocabulary that unites individuals across diverse backgrounds. Whether drawn from ancient philosophies, classic literature, or contemporary thought leaders, these quotes become bridges that connect people through shared experiences, aspirations, and the collective pursuit of a purposeful life.

The Art of Curating Inspiration

Diverse Voices, Universal Themes: Curating inspiration involves exploring the rich tapestry of diverse voices that contribute to the collective wisdom of humanity. Inspirational quotes sourced from a variety of sources—philosophers, writers, activists, spiritual leaders—encompass universal themes such as resilience, love, purpose, and the human capacity for growth. The inclusion of diverse voices enriches the mosaic of inspiration, offering a kaleidoscope of perspectives.

Aligning Quotes with Personal Values: Effectively curating inspiration requires aligning quotes with personal values and aspirations. Inspirational quotes serve as touchstones for individuals to reconnect with their core beliefs and principles. When curated thoughtfully, these quotes become not only sources of motivation but also anchors that ground individuals in the values that define their purposeful journey.

Dynamic Curation for Evolving Journeys: As individuals evolve on their life journeys, the relevance of inspirational quotes may shift. Dynamic curation involves an ongoing process of exploration and discovery, allowing individuals to update their collection of quotes to align with their current aspirations and challenges. The act of dynamic curation reflects the fluidity of personal growth and the adaptive nature of purposeful living.

Themes in Inspirational Quotes

Resilience in the Face of Challenges: Inspirational quotes often touch upon the theme of resilience—the ability to bounce back from adversity, face challenges with strength, and persevere in the pursuit of one's goals. These quotes serve as reminders that setbacks are not the end of the journey but opportunities for growth and resilience.

Embracing Change and Transformation: Change is an inevitable part of life, and many inspirational quotes revolve around the theme of embracing change and transformation. Whether advocating for the acceptance of impermanence or encouraging individuals to actively seek growth, these quotes guide individuals in navigating the evolving landscapes of their lives.

The Power of Purposeful Action: Action lies at the heart of purposeful living, and inspirational quotes often emphasize the transformative power of intentional, purpose-driven actions. Quotes in this theme inspire individuals to take meaningful steps, make conscious choices, and contribute positively to their own lives and the world around them.

Integrating Inspirational Quotes into Daily Life

Morning Reflections and Affirmations: Inspirational quotes find a natural home in morning reflections and affirmations. Starting the day with carefully chosen words sets a positive tone, offering a mental and emotional anchor for the day ahead. Whether through meditation, journaling, or simply repeating affirmations, individuals integrate the power of inspirational quotes into their daily rituals.

Visual Reminders in Personal Spaces: The physical environment plays a significant role in shaping thoughts and emotions. Integrating inspirational quotes into personal spaces—on walls, desks, or as screensavers—creates visual reminders of guiding principles. These visual cues serve as constant touchstones, subtly influencing mindset and fostering an environment conducive to purposeful living.

Inspirational Quotes as Mantras: Transforming inspirational quotes into personal mantras involves not only reciting them but embodying their essence. Turning a quote into a mantra means allowing its wisdom to permeate thoughts, actions, and decision-making. Inspirational mantras become guiding lights, influencing behavior and fostering alignment with one's purpose.

The Impact of Language on Mindset

Language and Mindset: The language individuals use, both internally and externally, shapes their mindset. Inspirational quotes act as linguistic architects, constructing mental frameworks that support positive thinking and resilience. The impact of language on mindset extends beyond momentary motivation, influencing long-term perspectives and the cultivation of a purpose-oriented mindset.

Reframing Challenges Through Language: Inspirational quotes provide a linguistic toolkit for reframing challenges. When faced with difficulties, individuals can draw upon the wisdom encapsulated in these quotes to shift their perspective. The act of reframing challenges through language becomes a strategy for maintaining optimism, resilience, and a sense of purpose amid life's inevitable ups and downs.

Words as Seeds of Manifestation: The principle of manifestation suggests that thoughts and words have the power to shape one's reality. Inspirational quotes, when embraced with conviction, act as seeds of manifestation. The intentional use of positive, purpose-driven language aligns thoughts and actions with the envisioned reality, creating a pathway for the manifestation of purposeful outcomes.

Rituals for Deepening Connection with Quotes

Reflective Journaling: Reflective journaling becomes a ritual for deepening one's connection with inspirational quotes. Taking the time to journal thoughts and reflections on a chosen quote enhances the process of internalization. Journaling allows individuals to explore the personal significance of a quote, uncovering layers of meaning and insights.

Shared Reflections in Community: Sharing reflections on inspirational quotes within a community setting creates a collective reservoir of wisdom and support. Whether in book clubs, discussion groups, or online forums, communal reflection on quotes fosters a shared language of inspiration. The diversity of perspectives within a community enriches the collective understanding of the quotes' meanings.

Incorporating Quotes Into Meditation Practices: Incorporating inspirational quotes into meditation practices deepens the connection between language and inner stillness. During meditation, individuals can focus on a chosen quote, allowing its resonance to permeate their consciousness. This integration of quotes into meditative moments becomes a ritual for cultivating a sense of peace, clarity, and purpose.

Conclusion: Quotes as Illuminators on the Path

As we conclude our exploration of inspirational quotes, let the resonance of these carefully chosen words linger—a reminder that language has the power to illuminate the path to purpose.

May the exploration of inspirational quotes be an illumination—a mindful interplay of language, wisdom, and the continuous alignment with purpose. As we transition to the subsequent chapters, may the spirit of inspirational quotes resonate—an invitation to immerse oneself in the transformative power of language, draw inspiration from the collective wisdom of humanity, and continue to tread the path with words as steadfast companions.

Uplifting Music Playlists

In the symphony of life, music possesses a unique power to stir emotions, evoke memories, and, most importantly, serve as a guiding force on the journey of purposeful living. This chapter explores the role of uplifting music playlists as touchstones—curated collections of songs that inspire, uplift, and resonate with the deeper meaning behind individual pursuits. As we delve into this theme, we uncover the transformative influence of music on mindset, emotions, and the continuous alignment with purpose.

The Language of Music

Emotions Unveiled in Melody: Music, as a universal language, has the unparalleled ability to unveil and express a myriad of emotions. The interplay of melody, harmony, and rhythm becomes a canvas on which the human experience is painted with intricate strokes of joy, sorrow, hope, and determination. Uplifting music playlists harness this emotional palette, offering individuals a means to connect with their innermost feelings and find resonance with the essence of their purpose.

Rhythmic Resonance with the Soul: The rhythmic heartbeat of music resonates with the very essence of the human soul. Uplifting music playlists tap into the primal connection between rhythm and life, providing a sonic backdrop that mirrors the pulsating energy within. The synchronization of heartbeat with music becomes a ritualistic dance—an intimate communion with the life force that propels individuals forward on their purposeful journeys.

Soundtracks of Memory and Meaning: Music acts as a powerful mnemonic device, imprinting memories and experiences with profound emotional significance. Uplifting music playlists become soundtracks of memory and meaning, weaving together the threads of personal history and purpose. The resonance of specific songs with pivotal moments serves as a touchstone, evoking the emotions and motivations that underpin the pursuit of a purposeful life.

The Art of Curating Uplifting Music Playlists

Diverse Genres, Singular Vibes: Curating uplifting music playlists involves exploring a diverse range of genres, each with its unique sonic landscape. From classical compositions to contemporary beats, the inclusion of diverse genres creates a tapestry of musical experiences. The common thread running through these genres is the singular vibe—an uplifting resonance that transcends stylistic boundaries and resonates with the soul.

Lyrics as Poetic Affirmations: The lyrics of a song carry the power of poetic affirmations, encapsulating themes of resilience, love, hope, and purpose. Curating uplifting music playlists involves a discerning selection of songs with lyrics that align with personal values and aspirations. The marriage of melody and meaningful lyrics amplifies the impact of the playlist, turning it into a reservoir of positive affirmations.

Dynamic Playlists for Dynamic Journeys: As life unfolds with its twists and turns, the relevance of certain songs may evolve. Dynamic curation involves an ongoing process of updating and refining uplifting music playlists to align with the current chapter of one's life journey. The adaptability of playlists mirrors the dynamic nature of personal growth and the ever-changing landscapes of purpose.

Themes in Uplifting Music Playlists

Songs of Resilience: Uplifting music playlists often feature songs that narrate stories of resilience—the triumph over adversity, the strength found in vulnerability, and the unwavering spirit in the face of challenges. These songs become anthems of fortitude, serving as touchstones that remind individuals of their own capacity to overcome obstacles on the path to purpose.

Melodies of Hope and Positivity: Hope is a driving force on the journey of purposeful living, and many uplifting music playlists are adorned with melodies that exude positivity and hope. Whether through upbeat rhythms, uplifting choruses, or lyrics that paint a brighter tomorrow, these songs become sonic beacons, guiding individuals towards an optimistic mindset and a sense of purpose.

Anthems of Love and Connection: Love, in its various forms, is a central theme in many uplifting music playlists. Whether celebrating romantic love, platonic connections, or the universal love for humanity, these songs resonate with the essence of purposeful living—forging meaningful connections and contributing positively to the world. Love becomes a touchstone that anchors individuals in the interconnectedness of life.

Integrating Uplifting Music Playlists into Daily Life

Morning Melodies for Positive Starts: Uplifting music playlists find a natural home in the morning routine, setting the tone for the day ahead. Starting the day with positive melodies creates a mental and emotional foundation that influences mindset and outlook. Morning melodies become a ritual for beginning each day with a sense of purpose, joy, and optimism.

Communal Listening for Shared Vibes: Sharing uplifting music playlists within communities—whether among friends, family, or online groups—creates a shared sonic space. Communal listening sessions become rituals for fostering connection, shared energy, and a collective upliftment of spirits. The diversity of musical tastes within a community enriches the collective experience, creating a harmonious blend of individual preferences.

Musical Affirmations in Creative Spaces: Integrating uplifting music playlists into creative spaces—whether at work, during artistic pursuits, or in personal sanctuaries—enhances the atmosphere with positive vibrations. The playlist becomes a musical affirmation, infusing the environment with energy that supports focus, creativity, and a sense of purpose. Musical affirmations become a ritual for cultivating an uplifting ambiance in daily life.

The Impact of Music on Mindset

Mood Elevation Through Melody: The impact of music on mood is a well-documented phenomenon. Uplifting music playlists act as mood elevators, influencing emotions and mindset. The power of melody to uplift spirits, evoke joy, and induce positive emotions becomes a touchstone for maintaining a resilient and purpose-oriented mindset.

Music as a Catalyst for Mindfulness: Listening to music mindfully, fully engaging with the sounds and sensations, becomes a form of musical meditation. Uplifting music playlists, when approached with mindfulness, serve as catalysts for staying present in the moment. The rhythmic journey of the music becomes a vehicle for grounding individuals in the now and fostering a sense of purposeful awareness.

The Language of Music and Visualization: Music has the ability to evoke vivid mental images and emotions. Uplifting music playlists, when coupled with visualization techniques, become a potent tool for manifesting positive outcomes. The symbiosis of music and visualization becomes a ritual for aligning mental imagery with purpose, creating a powerful synergy between sonic and visual affirmations.

Rituals for Deepening Connection with Uplifting Music Playlists

Sonic Journaling: Sonic journaling involves reflecting on the emotional and mental responses evoked by specific songs in an uplifting music playlist. Keeping a sonic journal becomes a ritual for exploring the connections between music, emotions, and personal reflections. Sonic journaling allows individuals to deepen their understanding of the songs that serve as touchstones on their purposeful journey.

Musical Mindfulness Meditation: Incorporating uplifting music playlists into mindfulness meditation practices enhances the meditative experience. Focusing on the sounds, rhythms, and melodies during meditation creates a harmonious space for inner exploration and alignment with purpose. Musical mindfulness meditation becomes a ritual for cultivating a centered and purposeful state of being.

Dance as a Form of Musical Expression: Engaging in dance as a form of musical expression transforms the listening experience into a physical ritual. Dancing to uplifting music playlists becomes a celebration of life, a joyful expression of purpose, and a ritual for embodying the energy and vibrancy of the music. Dance becomes a language of the soul, allowing individuals to physically connect with the guiding force of purpose.

Conclusion: Melodies as Guides on the Harmonious Path

As we conclude our exploration of uplifting music playlists, let the melodies linger—a reminder that music has the power to harmonize the journey to purpose.

May the exploration of uplifting music playlists be a harmonious interplay of melody, emotion, and the continuous alignment with purpose. As we transition to the subsequent chapters, may the spirit of uplifting music resonate—an invitation to immerse oneself in the transformative power of sonic affirmations, draw inspiration from the universal language of music, and continue to tread the path with melodies as steadfast companions.

Support Networks

In the intricate tapestry of a purposeful life, the threads of connection form an essential element, weaving together a network of support that sustains, uplifts, and reinforces the journey toward fulfillment. This chapter delves into the significance of support networks as touchstones—interpersonal connections that serve as pillars of strength, guidance, and encouragement. As we explore this theme, we unravel the dynamics of building, nurturing, and leveraging support networks on the path to purpose.

The Essence of Support Networks

Interdependence in the Human Experience: At the core of human existence lies the undeniable truth of interdependence. Individuals are not solitary entities but interconnected beings, and support networks acknowledge and embody this interdependence. These networks signify a shared journey where each person contributes to the collective well-being, fostering an environment where the pursuit of purpose becomes a collaborative endeavor.

Shared Wisdom and Collective Resilience: Support networks act as repositories of shared wisdom, collective experiences, and diverse perspectives. Within these networks, individuals find a wellspring of insights, advice, and lessons learned, collectively contributing to the resilience of the group. The diversity of experiences within a support network becomes a touchstone for navigating challenges, embracing growth, and continually aligning with purpose.

Emotional Anchors in the Journey: Emotions, integral to the human experience, find solace and expression within the framework of support networks. These networks become emotional anchors, providing a safe space for individuals to share their joys, struggles, and vulnerabilities. The reciprocal nature of emotional support within the network creates touchstones that stabilize individuals amid life's fluctuating circumstances.

The Art of Cultivating Support Networks

Intentional Relationship Building: Cultivating support networks requires intentional and mindful relationship building. Individuals embark on a purposeful journey of connecting with others who share similar values, aspirations, and a commitment to mutual growth. Intentionality becomes a touchstone, guiding individuals to seek and nurture relationships that contribute positively to their pursuit of purpose.

Reciprocity as the Heartbeat of Connection: Reciprocity forms the heartbeat of meaningful connections within support networks. The give-and-take dynamics create a sense of balance, trust, and mutual benefit. Reciprocal relationships become touchstones for individuals, reminding them of the power of shared efforts, mutual encouragement, and the collaborative energy that propels everyone forward on the journey.

Dynamic Networks for Dynamic Lives: As individuals evolve, so too do their needs and aspirations. Dynamic support networks adapt to the changing landscapes of individuals' lives, accommodating shifts in priorities, goals, and personal growth. The dynamism within the network becomes a touchstone, ensuring that the support structure remains relevant, supportive, and aligned with the ever-evolving nature of purpose.

Themes in Support Networks

Mentorship and Guidance: Mentorship within support networks serves as a guiding touchstone on the journey to purpose. Mentors, individuals with wisdom and experience, offer valuable insights, advice, and encouragement. The mentor-mentee dynamic becomes a symbiotic relationship, with both parties contributing to each other's growth and navigating the path of purpose together.

Empathy and Understanding: Empathy is the currency of connection within support networks. The ability to understand and resonate with the experiences of others fosters a culture of compassion and mutual support. Empathetic connections become touchstones, providing a sense of understanding, validation, and shared humanity on the quest for purpose.

Celebrating Successes and Milestones: Support networks serve as cheerleaders during moments of success and celebration. Whether big achievements or small victories, the collective joy within the network becomes a touchstone for acknowledging progress, fostering a positive mindset, and reinforcing the belief that individual successes contribute to the greater tapestry of the group.

Integrating Support Networks into Daily Life

Regular Check-ins and Communication: Integrating support networks into daily life involves regular check-ins and open communication. These practices become touchstones for maintaining strong connections, staying informed about each other's journeys, and offering timely support when needed. Regular communication ensures that the network remains a vibrant and responsive part of individuals' lives.

Collaborative Goal Setting: Support networks become touchstones for collaborative goal setting. Individuals within the network can align their aspirations, set shared goals, and work collectively toward their fulfillment. Collaborative goal setting fosters a sense of accountability, shared purpose, and a dynamic synergy that propels everyone forward.

Mutual Accountability and Growth: Mutual accountability within support networks becomes a touchstone for personal and collective growth. Individuals hold each other accountable for the commitments they make toward their purposeful pursuits. This shared accountability creates a supportive structure that encourages consistent progress and resilience amid challenges.

The Impact of Support Networks on Mindset

Positive Influence on Outlook: Support networks wield a profound influence on mindset, shaping individuals' outlook on life and their journey toward purpose. Positive connections, encouragement, and shared experiences within the network become touchstones for fostering an optimistic mindset. The collective positivity acts as a powerful force that counterbalances challenges and cultivates a resilient attitude.

Confidence and Self-Efficacy: The belief in one's ability to navigate challenges and achieve goals, known as self-efficacy, is bolstered within support networks. Encouragement, feedback, and shared successes within the network become touchstones for building confidence. The collective belief in each other's capabilities becomes a source of strength that propels individuals toward purposeful actions.

Emotional Well-being and Resilience: Emotional well-being is closely intertwined with the strength of support networks. The emotional support, understanding, and empathy within the network become touchstones for resilience. In times of difficulty, individuals draw on the emotional reservoir within the network, finding solace, encouragement, and a renewed sense of purpose.

Rituals for Deepening Connection within Support Networks

Shared Reflections and Wisdom Circles: Creating space for shared reflections and wisdom circles within support networks becomes a ritual for deepening connection. Whether through regular meetings, virtual gatherings, or written reflections, these rituals provide a platform for individuals to share insights, lessons learned, and the wisdom gained on their respective journeys.

Mutual Celebrations and Gratitude Practices: Incorporating mutual celebrations and gratitude practices within support networks becomes a ritual for fostering a culture of appreciation. Recognizing and celebrating each other's successes, milestones, and contributions becomes a touchstone for gratitude. These rituals reinforce the positive energy within the network and deepen the sense of shared purpose.

Supportive Rituals During Challenges: In times of challenge, support networks can establish supportive rituals to provide comfort and encouragement. Whether through shared virtual rituals, supportive messages, or collaborative problem-solving sessions, these rituals become touchstones for navigating difficulties as a collective force.

Conclusion: Networks as Pillars on the Purposeful Path

As we conclude our exploration of support networks, let the interconnected threads linger—a reminder that the strength of connections forms pillars on the path to purpose.

May the exploration of support networks be an interwoven tapestry—a mindful interplay of connections, shared wisdom, and the continuous alignment with purpose. As we transition to the subsequent chapters, may the spirit of support networks resonate—an invitation to cultivate and cherish meaningful connections, draw inspiration from collective strength, and continue to tread the path with supportive networks as steadfast companions.

Conclusion
Progress Over Perfection

In the final verses of our exploration into the realms of purposeful living, it becomes essential to reflect on a foundational principle that underscores the entire journey—an ethos that serves as a guiding light and a touchstone for those traversing the path: Progress Over Perfection. In these closing thoughts, we delve into the profound wisdom encapsulated in these three words and unravel the significance of embracing progress as a constant companion on the purposeful journey.

The Paralysis of Perfection

The Illusion of Perfect Endings: Perfection, with its allure of flawlessness and completion, often masquerades as an ideal destination. It whispers promises of unattainable standards, where every goal is flawlessly achieved, every intention perfectly realized, and every facet of life seamlessly aligned. However, this pursuit of a perfect ending can become a mirage, leading to a sense of disillusionment and stagnation.

The Weight of Unrealistic Expectations: The quest for perfection carries the burden of unrealistic expectations. Individuals striving for an unblemished outcome may find themselves ensnared in the web of impossibly high standards. The weight of these expectations can cast a shadow over achievements, overshadowing progress with the relentless pursuit of flawlessness.

Perfection as a Moving Target: Perfection, when viewed as an endpoint, becomes a moving target—a destination that constantly recedes with each step taken towards it. The ever-elusive nature of perfection can breed frustration, anxiety, and a perpetual sense of inadequacy. The pursuit of an idealized version of life can overshadow the beauty inherent in the imperfect, ever-evolving nature of the human experience.

The Liberating Power of Progress

Acknowledging the Journey: In contrast to the rigid demands of perfection, progress invites individuals to acknowledge and celebrate the journey itself. It is a recognition that life is a dynamic, evolving narrative, where each step forward, regardless of its size, contributes to the unfolding story. Embracing progress involves a mindful shift from fixating on the destination to appreciating the transformative power embedded in the journey.

Learning Through Iterations: Progress unfolds through iterations, a series of learning experiences, adjustments, and adaptations. The iterative nature of progress allows individuals to refine their goals, intentions, and actions based on insights gained along the way. Each iteration becomes a touchstone for growth—a reminder that the journey is not a linear path but a rich tapestry of experiences that contribute to personal evolution.

Embracing the Imperfect Beauty: Progress invites individuals to embrace the imperfect beauty of the present moment. It acknowledges that life, with all its twists and turns, is a mosaic of successes, setbacks, and ongoing growth. The imperfect nature of progress becomes a touchstone for authenticity, self-compassion, and an appreciation for the uniqueness inherent in each person's journey.

The Dynamics of Purposeful Progress

Aligned Actions and Intentions: Progress in the context of purposeful living involves aligning actions with intentions. It is not about achieving a predetermined state of perfection but about consistently taking steps that resonate with one's values, aspirations, and sense of purpose. Aligned actions become touchstones, guiding individuals toward a life that reflects their true essence.

Course Corrections and Flexibility: The journey of purpose is marked by an inherent flexibility—a willingness to adapt and make course corrections as needed. Progress, in this context, involves navigating the inevitable twists and turns with resilience and an openness to growth. The ability to pivot in response to changing circumstances becomes a touchstone for staying true to purpose amid the ebb and flow of life.

Celebrating Milestones, Big and Small: Progress invites individuals to celebrate milestones, both big and small, along the way. These milestones serve as touchstones, markers of personal growth, and reminders of the progress made. Celebrations become rituals of acknowledgment, fostering a positive mindset and reinforcing the belief in one's capacity to continue moving forward.

Integrating Progress Over Perfection into Daily Life

Mindful Reflection on Progress: Integrating progress over perfection into daily life involves mindful reflection on one's journey. Regular pauses for introspection allow individuals to recognize and appreciate the progress made, no matter how incremental. Mindful reflection becomes a touchstone for cultivating self-awareness and a sense of gratitude for the ongoing journey.

Cultivating a Growth Mindset: Progress is closely intertwined with a growth mindset—a belief that abilities and intelligence can be developed through dedication and hard work. Cultivating a growth mindset involves viewing challenges as opportunities for learning, embracing feedback, and seeing effort as a path to mastery. A growth mindset becomes a touchstone for continuous improvement on the purposeful path.

Self-Compassion Amid Setbacks: In the pursuit of progress, setbacks are inevitable. Integrating progress over perfection into daily life requires cultivating self-compassion when facing challenges. Recognizing setbacks as opportunities for learning, reframing failures as stepping stones, and extending kindness to oneself become touchstones for resilience and a positive mindset.

The Impact of Embracing Progress

A Positive Impact on Well-Being: Embracing progress over perfection has a profound impact on overall well-being. The focus on continuous improvement, learning, and growth contributes to a positive mindset, reduced stress, and increased life satisfaction. The journey becomes a source of fulfillment, with progress serving as a touchstone for a flourishing and purposeful life.

Enhanced Resilience in the Face of Challenges: Progress-oriented individuals exhibit enhanced resilience when facing challenges. The ability to view difficulties as opportunities for growth, coupled with a belief in one's capacity to overcome obstacles, becomes a touchstone for navigating adversity. The journey becomes a testament to the strength cultivated through the pursuit of progress.

Fostering a Sense of Purposeful Momentum: Embracing progress over perfection fosters a sense of purposeful momentum. Each step forward becomes a building block for the next, creating a continuous flow of energy and enthusiasm for the journey. The momentum becomes a touchstone, propelling individuals forward on the path to purpose with a sense of purposeful urgency.

Rituals for Embracing Progress

Journaling the Journey: Keeping a journal becomes a ritual for documenting the journey of progress. Regular entries allow individuals to reflect on the steps taken, milestones achieved, and lessons learned. Journaling becomes a touchstone for self-discovery, providing a tangible record of the ongoing evolution on the purposeful path.

Vision Boards as Visual Touchstones: Creating vision boards becomes a ritual for visualizing progress. These visual touchstones serve as tangible representations of goals, intentions, and the envisioned future self. Vision boards become a source of inspiration, reminding individuals of the progress they aspire to make and the purpose that propels them forward.

Gratitude Practices for Acknowledgment: Incorporating gratitude practices becomes a ritual for acknowledging progress. Expressing gratitude for the journey, the lessons learned, and the growth experienced becomes a touchstone for cultivating a positive mindset. Gratitude practices reinforce the awareness that progress is an ongoing and meaningful aspect of the purposeful path.

Conclusion: The Symphony of Progress

As we conclude our exploration of progress over perfection, let the resonance of these words linger—a reminder that progress is not a destination but a symphony that accompanies the purposeful journey.

May the exploration of progress over perfection be a harmonious interplay of growth, self-compassion, and the continuous alignment with purpose. As we transition from these reflections to the greater tapestry of life, may the spirit of progress resonate—an invitation to embrace the imperfect beauty of the journey, celebrate each step forward, and continue to tread the path with progress as a steadfast companion.

Flexibility Along the Path

In the final strokes of our journey through the landscapes of purposeful living, we turn our gaze to a fundamental aspect that shapes the contours of the path—Flexibility Along the Path. Within the dynamic tapestry of a purpose-driven life, the ability to embrace flexibility becomes a compass, guiding individuals through the ever-changing terrain of challenges, opportunities, and self-discovery. In these closing reflections, we explore the profound significance of flexibility as an intrinsic quality that not only enriches the journey but also becomes a touchstone for navigating the twists and turns inherent in the pursuit of purpose.

The Nature of a Flexible Mindset

Adapting to Change: Flexibility, at its essence, is the capacity to adapt to change. Life is inherently fluid, marked by unforeseen shifts in circumstances, priorities, and perspectives. A flexible mindset acknowledges the inevitability of change and responds with openness, resilience, and a willingness to adjust course as needed.

Embracing Uncertainty: The journey of purpose is often threaded with uncertainty—a terrain where the destination may not be clearly defined, and the path may unfold in unexpected ways. Flexibility involves embracing the uncertainty inherent in purposeful living, viewing it not as a barrier but as an invitation to explore, learn, and evolve.

Balancing Structure and Spontaneity: Flexibility strikes a delicate balance between structure and spontaneity. While structure provides a framework for intentional living and goal pursuit, spontaneity allows for creative exploration, adaptation, and the serendipitous moments that breathe life into the journey. The interplay between structure and spontaneity becomes a touchstone for a dynamic and vibrant existence.

The Pitfalls of Rigidity

The Stranglehold of Rigidity: In contrast to flexibility, rigidity manifests as a stranglehold—a resistance to deviation from predetermined plans, a fear of the unknown, and a reluctance to adapt. A rigid mindset can lead to stagnation, missed opportunities, and a sense of frustration when confronted with the inevitable uncertainties of life.

The Paralysis of Perfectionism: Rigidity often intertwines with perfectionism, creating a mindset where the pursuit of an idealized vision becomes the primary focus. This fixation on perfection can result in a narrow perspective, stifling creativity, and hindering the exploration of alternative paths that may lead to unexpected and fulfilling destinations.

Resistance to Growth: A rigid mindset resists the natural process of growth and transformation. Change, which is an integral aspect of personal development, becomes a source of discomfort rather than an opportunity for learning. The resistance to growth impedes the journey toward becoming one's best self and living with purpose.

The Liberating Power of Flexibility

Navigating Life's Detours: Life's journey is replete with detours—unexpected twists and turns that may lead individuals away from their initially charted course. Flexibility empowers individuals to navigate these detours with grace and adaptability, viewing them not as obstacles but as scenic routes that may reveal new perspectives and opportunities.

Learning from Setbacks: Setbacks are an inherent part of any journey, and a flexible mindset transforms setbacks into stepping stones for growth. Rather than viewing obstacles as insurmountable roadblocks, flexibility enables individuals to extract lessons, pivot when necessary, and approach challenges with a mindset of resilience and continuous learning.

Seizing Opportunities in Change: Change, often viewed with trepidation, becomes an ally when approached with flexibility. Rather than fearing the unknown, a flexible mindset allows individuals to embrace change as an opportunity for growth, discovery, and the unveiling of uncharted possibilities. Change becomes a touchstone for reinvention and the evolution of purpose.

The Dynamics of Flexibility on the Purposeful Path

Aligning with Core Values: Flexibility, when grounded in core values, becomes a guiding force on the purposeful path. While external circumstances may shift, the alignment with core values provides a stable foundation. Flexibility in the pursuit of purpose involves adapting strategies and plans while staying true to the fundamental principles that define one's journey.

Adapting Goals to Evolving Aspirations: The journey toward purpose is marked by evolving aspirations, and flexibility allows individuals to adapt their goals in response to these changes. Rather than rigidly adhering to initial plans, individuals with a flexible mindset recalibrate their goals, ensuring that they remain in harmony with their current understanding of purpose.

Integrating Mindfulness into Flexibility: Flexibility is closely intertwined with mindfulness—a heightened awareness of the present moment and an openness to the unfolding reality. The integration of mindfulness into flexibility becomes a touchstone for making intentional choices, responding thoughtfully to challenges, and maintaining a sense of equilibrium amid the ebb and flow of life.

Themes in Flexible Living

Resilience as a Pillar of Flexibility: Flexibility and resilience share a symbiotic relationship. A flexible mindset fosters resilience, enabling individuals to bounce back from setbacks, adapt to changing circumstances, and maintain a positive outlook in the face of adversity. Resilience becomes a touchstone for navigating the unpredictable nature of the purposeful journey.

Collaborative Flexibility in Relationships: Flexibility extends beyond individual mindsets to permeate the fabric of relationships. Collaborative flexibility involves navigating the intricacies of interpersonal dynamics with adaptability, empathy, and a willingness to find common ground. Flexibility in relationships becomes a touchstone for creating harmonious connections that support the collective pursuit of purpose.

Strategic Flexibility in Decision-Making: Strategic flexibility involves a nuanced approach to decision-making. It is the art of being adaptable while maintaining a strategic focus on long-term goals. This form of flexibility becomes a touchstone for making informed choices, adjusting plans as needed, and staying attuned to the overarching purpose that guides decision-making.

Integrating Flexibility into Daily Life

Mindful Decision-Making: Integrating flexibility into daily life begins with mindful decision-making. This involves a conscious awareness of the choices one makes, an openness to alternative possibilities, and a willingness to adjust plans when needed. Mindful decision-making becomes a touchstone for aligning daily actions with purpose.

Routine Adjustments for Dynamic Living: Flexibility within daily life includes making routine adjustments to accommodate the dynamic nature of purposeful living. Whether adapting daily routines to changing priorities or incorporating spontaneous moments of joy, routine adjustments become touchstones for infusing vitality into everyday existence.

Embracing the Unexpected: Flexibility invites individuals to embrace the unexpected with curiosity rather than fear. Whether faced with unexpected opportunities or challenges, the ability to adapt and respond with flexibility becomes a touchstone for turning the unexpected into avenues for growth, exploration, and discovery.

The Impact of a Flexible Mindset

Enhanced Adaptability in a Changing World: In a world marked by rapid change, a flexible mindset becomes a valuable asset. The ability to adapt to shifting landscapes, embrace uncertainty, and navigate change with resilience becomes a touchstone for thriving in a dynamic and evolving environment.

Reduction of Stress and Anxiety: A flexible mindset contributes to the reduction of stress and anxiety. Rather than feeling overwhelmed by the unpredictability of life, individuals with a flexible mindset approach challenges with a sense of adaptability and a belief in their capacity to navigate uncertainties. Flexibility becomes a touchstone for cultivating a calm and centered approach to life.

Fostering a Culture of Innovation: In both personal and professional realms, a flexible mindset fosters a culture of innovation. The openness to new ideas, the ability to pivot in response to feedback, and the willingness to experiment become touchstones for creative problem-solving and continuous improvement.

Rituals for Cultivating Flexibility

Daily Reflection on Flexibility: Cultivating flexibility involves incorporating daily reflection into one's routine. Taking a few moments each day to reflect on how flexibility was applied, the lessons learned, and areas for improvement becomes a ritual for reinforcing a flexible mindset. Daily reflection becomes a touchstone for continuous growth.

Mindfulness Practices for Flexibility: Mindfulness practices, such as meditation and deep breathing, become rituals for cultivating flexibility. These practices enhance self-awareness, reduce reactivity, and foster a calm presence in the face of challenges. Mindfulness becomes a touchstone for infusing flexibility into moments of daily life.

Intentional Adaptations in Goal Setting: Adapting goals with intentionality becomes a ritual for integrating flexibility into the pursuit of purpose. Regularly reassessing goals, considering new aspirations, and adjusting plans as needed become touchstones for aligning the journey with evolving visions of purpose.

Conclusion: The Dance of Flexibility

As we conclude our exploration of flexibility along the path, let the echoes of these reflections resonate—a reminder that flexibility is not a compromise but a dance—an artful navigation of the ever-changing rhythms of life.

May the exploration of flexibility be a dance—a graceful interplay of adaptability, resilience, and the continuous alignment with purpose. As we transition from these reflections to the greater symphony of existence, may the spirit of flexibility resonate—an invitation to embrace the dynamic nature of the journey, navigate challenges with grace, and continue to tread the path with flexibility as a steadfast companion.

Transformation as a Continuum

In the final chapters of our expedition through the realms of purposeful living, we turn our gaze to a concept that encapsulates the very essence of the journey—Transformation as a Continuum. As we navigate the rich landscapes of personal growth, self-discovery, and intentional living, the understanding that transformation is not a finite destination but an ongoing, dynamic process becomes a guiding principle. In these concluding reflections, we explore the profound depth of transformation as a continuum, delving into the ways it shapes our understanding of self, purpose, and the evolving narrative of a purpose-driven life.

The Nature of Transformation

Dynamic Unfolding: Transformation, when viewed as a continuum, is a dynamic unfolding—a perpetual evolution of self, mindset, and life circumstances. Rather than a static state to be reached, it is an ongoing journey that weaves its way through the fabric of daily experiences, challenges, and the intentional choices that shape the narrative of our lives.

Integration of Experiences: A continuum of transformation involves the integration of experiences—both triumphs and setbacks—into the tapestry of personal growth. Each experience becomes a thread, contributing to the complex and beautiful mosaic of the evolving self. The integration of experiences becomes a touchstone for cultivating resilience, wisdom, and a deeper understanding of one's purpose.

Cyclical Nature of Growth: Transformation as a continuum embraces the cyclical nature of growth. It acknowledges that the journey is marked by seasons of expansion, flourishing, and abundance, as well as seasons of contraction, introspection, and rejuvenation. The cyclical nature becomes a touchstone for understanding that periods of rest and reflection are integral to the overall rhythm of transformation.

The Pitfalls of a Destination Mentality

The Illusion of Arrival: A destination mentality perceives transformation as an endpoint—an illusionary arrival at a state of perfection, enlightenment, or ultimate fulfillment. This mindset can create a sense of disillusionment when the anticipated destination is not met, overlooking the richness inherent in the ongoing journey of transformation.

Rigidity in Self-Concept: A destination-oriented perspective can lead to rigidity in self-concept. Individuals may cling to a fixed image of who they should become or what their lives should look like once transformation is deemed complete. This rigidity inhibits the fluidity necessary for embracing the ever-changing nature of personal growth.

Missed Opportunities for Learning: When transformation is viewed as a destination, opportunities for learning and growth within everyday experiences may be overlooked. The emphasis on reaching a specific point may overshadow the invaluable lessons embedded in the journey itself. The continuous process of learning becomes a touchstone for growth-oriented individuals.

Embracing Transformation as a Continuum

The Beauty of Becoming: Embracing transformation as a continuum allows individuals to appreciate the beauty of becoming—the joy found in the journey itself. It shifts the focus from a distant destination to the present moment, inviting a deep appreciation for the process of unfolding, learning, and becoming one's best self.

A Mindset of Growth: A continuum of transformation is synonymous with a growth mindset—an outlook that sees challenges as opportunities for learning, embraces effort as a path to mastery, and views setbacks as stepping stones toward improvement. A growth mindset becomes a touchstone for cultivating resilience and a positive perspective on the journey.

Evolution of Purpose: As transformation unfolds along a continuum, so too does the evolution of purpose. The understanding of one's purpose becomes a dynamic exploration, adapting to changing aspirations, values, and life circumstances. The evolution of purpose becomes a touchstone for aligning daily actions with a sense of meaning and fulfillment.

The Dynamics of Transformation on the Purposeful Path

Self-Discovery as a Lifelong Journey: On the purposeful path, self-discovery is not a one-time revelation but a lifelong journey. Each chapter of life unfolds new layers of self-awareness, unveiling previously unseen facets of identity, values, and passions. Self-discovery becomes a touchstone for aligning personal growth with the pursuit of purpose.

Integrating Challenges into Growth: Challenges, rather than obstacles to be overcome, become integral components of growth on the purposeful path.

Transformation as a continuum involves integrating challenges into the narrative, reframing difficulties as opportunities for learning, resilience, and the development of character. Challenges become touchstones for fortitude and self-discovery.

Adapting Goals to Align with Evolving Purpose: Transformation along the purposeful path involves an ongoing dialogue between goals and evolving purpose. Rather than adhering rigidly to predefined objectives, individuals adapt their goals in response to the ever-deepening understanding of purpose. Adapting goals becomes a touchstone for aligning aspirations with the evolving narrative of a purpose-driven life.

Themes in a Continuous Transformation

Cultivating Mindfulness in the Present Moment: Embracing transformation as a continuum requires cultivating mindfulness in the present moment. It involves a heightened awareness of the here and now, an appreciation for the richness of daily experiences, and a conscious presence in the unfolding journey. Mindfulness becomes a touchstone for savoring the transformative nature of each moment.

Resilience Amid Uncertainty: A continuous transformation mindset fosters resilience in the face of uncertainty. Rather than fearing the unknown, individuals navigate uncertainty with adaptability, viewing it as an inherent aspect of the transformative journey. Resilience becomes a touchstone for navigating the ebb and flow of life with grace and fortitude.

Celebrating Milestones and Progress: Transformation as a continuum invites individuals to celebrate milestones and progress along the way. Rather than reserving acknowledgment for the attainment of specific destinations, individuals recognize and celebrate the continuous progress made on the journey. Celebrations become touchstones for gratitude and positive reinforcement.

Integrating Continuous Transformation into Daily Life

Reflective Practices for Ongoing Growth: Daily life becomes enriched when reflective practices are incorporated into the routine. Regular self-reflection, journaling, and mindfulness practices become rituals for ongoing growth. Reflective practices become touchstones for staying attuned to the evolving self and purpose.

Adapting Plans with Intentionality: Integrating continuous transformation into daily life involves adapting plans with intentionality. Whether recalibrating goals, adjusting strategies, or embracing unexpected opportunities, intentional adaptations become touchstones for aligning daily actions with the evolving narrative of purpose.

Cultivating a Curious Mindset: A curious mindset becomes a daily practice in continuous transformation. Approaching each day with curiosity, a willingness to explore new possibilities, and an openness to learning becomes a touchstone for infusing daily life with the spirit of ongoing transformation.

The Impact of Continuous Transformation

Enhanced Resilience in the Face of Change: Individuals who embrace continuous transformation exhibit enhanced resilience in the face of change. The ability to adapt, learn, and grow amid shifting circumstances becomes a touchstone for navigating the uncertainties of life with a sense of inner strength and equanimity.

Deeper Sense of Purposeful Living: Continuous transformation deepens the sense of purposeful living. The ongoing commitment to personal growth, self-discovery, and alignment with purpose becomes a touchstone for infusing daily life with meaning, fulfillment, and a sense of connection to a greater narrative.

A Holistic Approach to Well-Being: A continuous transformation mindset extends beyond personal development to encompass a holistic approach to well-being. Mental, emotional, and physical well-being become interconnected aspects of the transformative journey. Well-being becomes a touchstone for sustaining the energy and vitality needed for continuous growth.

Rituals for Embracing Continuous Transformation

Daily Reflection on the Journey: Cultivating a mindset of continuous transformation involves incorporating daily reflection into one's routine. Taking time each day to reflect on the day's experiences, lessons learned, and areas for growth becomes a ritual for reinforcing the understanding that transformation is an ongoing journey. Daily reflection becomes a touchstone for staying connected to the transformative nature of each day.

Regular Goal Assessments: Integrating continuous transformation into daily life includes regular assessments of goals. Rather than viewing goals as static endpoints, individuals assess their goals regularly, ensuring they remain aligned with evolving aspirations and purpose. Regular goal assessments become touchstones for intentional growth.

Commitment to Lifelong Learning: Continuous transformation thrives on a commitment to lifelong learning. Embracing new knowledge, skills, and perspectives becomes a ritual for staying adaptive and responsive to the ever-changing landscape of personal growth. Lifelong learning becomes a touchstone for a vibrant and intellectually stimulating journey.

Conclusion: A Symphony of Becoming

As we conclude our exploration of transformation as a continuum, let the echoes of these reflections linger—an invitation to dance with the symphony of becoming. May the understanding that transformation is an ongoing journey, a dynamic unfolding, resonate within—the melody of growth playing in harmony with the rhythm of purpose.

May the exploration of continuous transformation be a symphony—a celebration of becoming, evolving, and embracing the richness of the journey. As we transition from these reflections to the greater symphony of existence, may the spirit of continuous transformation resonate—an invitation to dance with the ongoing rhythms of purpose, growth, and the beautiful continuum of becoming.

THE END

Wordbook

Welcome to the glossary section of this book. Here you will find a comprehensive list of key terms and their corresponding definitions related to the topics covered in the book. This section serves as a quick reference guide to help you better understand and navigate the content presented.

1. Intentions: The purposeful and deliberate mental attitudes or plans, often set with the aim of guiding behavior and achieving desired outcomes.

2. Self-Fulfillment: The process of realizing one's full potential, achieving personal goals, and experiencing a deep sense of satisfaction and contentment.

3. Habits: Regular and repeated behaviors that become ingrained over time, shaping one's character and influencing daily actions.

4. Practices: Consistent and intentional activities or rituals designed to cultivate specific skills, attitudes, or states of mind.

5. Thriving: Flourishing or prospering in various aspects of life, including mental, emotional, and physical well-being.

6. The Science Behind Transformation: Understanding the psychological, physiological, and behavioral mechanisms that contribute to personal change and growth.

7. Crafting an Envisioned Future Self: Deliberately creating a mental image of the ideal version of oneself, serving as a guide for personal development.

8. Sustaining Growth Through Ritual: Fostering continuous personal development by incorporating intentional and meaningful practices into daily life.

9. Goals: Specific, measurable, and achievable objectives that individuals set to guide their efforts and measure progress.

10. Affirmations: Positive statements or declarations aimed at fostering a positive mindset, self-confidence, and motivation.

11. Gratitude: A state of appreciation and thankfulness for the positive aspects of life, fostering a positive outlook and well-being.

12. Mindfulness: The practice of being fully present and engaged in the current moment, enhancing awareness and reducing stress.

13. Positivity: A mental attitude characterized by an optimistic and constructive outlook, influencing one's perception and response to life.

14. Movement: Physical activities, including exercise, yoga, and dance, that contribute to overall well-being and positive mental states.

15. Healthy Eating: Consuming nutritious foods that contribute to physical health and mental clarity.

16. Creativity: The ability to generate novel ideas, solutions, or expressions, contributing to personal growth and fulfillment.

17. Expression: The act of conveying one's thoughts, feelings, or creativity through various forms, such as art, writing, or communication.

18. Touchstones: Symbolic reminders or guiding principles that serve as anchors for maintaining focus, purpose, and motivation.

19. Flexibility: An adaptive mindset and willingness to adjust plans, perspectives, and behaviors in response to changing circumstances.

20. Transformation: A profound and ongoing process of personal change, growth, and development towards a more purposeful and fulfilled life.

Supplementary Materials

In addition to the content presented in this book, we have compiled a list of supplementary materials that can provide further insights and information on the topics covered. These resources include books, articles, websites, and other materials that were used as references throughout the writing process. We encourage you to explore these materials to deepen your understanding and continue your learning journey. Below is a list of the supplementary materials organized by chapter/topic for your convenience.

Introduction

Dweck, C. S. (2006). Mindset: The New Psychology of Success. Ballantine Books.

Csikszentmihalyi, M. (2008). Flow: The Psychology of Optimal Experience. Harper Perennial Modern Classics.

Deci, E. L., & Ryan, R. M. (2000). "The 'what' and 'why' of goal pursuits: Human needs and the self-determination of behavior." Psychological Inquiry, 11(4), 227-268.

Chapter 1: Writing Down Goals and Affirmations

Locke, E. A., & Latham, G. P. (2002). "Building a practically useful theory of goal setting and task motivation: A 35-year odyssey." American Psychologist, 57(9), 705-717.

Cohen, G. L., Sherman, D. K., Bastardi, A., Hsu, L., & McGoey, M. (2007). "Leaving a legacy: Parting thoughts on the nature of generativity." Psychological Science, 18(6), 524-528.

Chapter 2: Cultivating Gratitude

Emmons, R. A., & McCullough, M. E. (2003). "Counting blessings versus burdens: An experimental investigation of gratitude and subjective well-being in daily life." Journal of Personality and Social Psychology, 84(2), 377-389.

Wood, A. M., Froh, J. J., & Geraghty, A. W. (2010). "Gratitude and well-being: A review and theoretical integration." Clinical Psychology Review, 30(7), 890-905.

Chapter 3: Practicing Mindfulness

Kabat-Zinn, J. (1994). Wherever You Go, There You Are: Mindfulness Meditation in Everyday Life. Hyperion.

Baer, R. A., Smith, G. T., Lykins, E., Button, D., Krietemeyer, J., Sauer, S., ... & Williams, J. M. (2008). "Construct validity of the five facet mindfulness questionnaire in meditating and nonmeditating samples." Assessment, 15(3), 329-342.

Chapter 4: Fueling Positivity Through Movement

Ratey, J. J. (2008). Spark: The Revolutionary New Science of Exercise and the Brain. Little, Brown Spark.

Särkämö, T., Tervaniemi, M., Laitinen, S., Forsblom, A., Soinila, S., Mikkonen, M., ... & Hietanen, M. (2008). "Music listening enhances cognitive recovery and mood after a middle cerebral artery stroke." Brain, 131(3), 866-876.

Chapter 5: Healthy Eating for Clarity

Wang, X., Ouyang, Y., Liu, J., Zhu, M., Zhao, G., Bao, W., & Hu, F. B. (2014). "Fruit and vegetable consumption and mortality from all causes, cardiovascular disease, and cancer: systematic review and dose-response meta-analysis of prospective cohort studies." British Medical Journal, 349, g4490.

Huo, R., Du, T., Xu, Y., Xu, W., Chen, X., Sun, K., & Yu, X. (2013). "Effects of Mediterranean-style diet on glycemic control, weight loss and cardiovascular risk factors among type 2 diabetes individuals: a meta-analysis." European Journal of Clinical Nutrition, 67(9), 1214-1219.

Chapter 6: Creative Expression

Csikszentmihalyi, M. (1996). Creativity: Flow and the Psychology of Discovery and Invention. Harper Collins.

Hanna, J. L. (1986). To Dance Is Human: A Theory of Nonverbal Communication. University of Chicago Press.

Chapter 7: Touchstones for Reminding Yourself of Purpose

Frankl, V. E. (2006). Man's Search for Meaning. Beacon Press.

Damasio, A. R. (1994). Descartes' Error: Emotion, Reason, and the Human Brain. Penguin Books.

Conclusion

Duckworth, A. L. (2016). Grit: The Power of Passion and Perseverance. Scribner.

Brown, B. (2012). Daring Greatly: How the Courage to Be Vulnerable Transforms the Way We Live, Love, Parent, and Lead. Avery.

www.ingramcontent.com/pod-product-compliance
Lightning Source LLC
LaVergne TN
LVHW012037070526
838202LV00056B/5524